Clara Barton

Clara Barton National Historic Site
Maryland

Produced by the
Division of Publications
National Park Service

U.S. Department of the Interior
Washington, D.C. 1981

D1342350

The National Park Handbook Series
National Park Handbooks, compact introductions to the
great natural and historic places administered by the
National Park Service, are designed to promote understanding and enjoyment of the parks. Each is intended
to be informative reading and a useful guide before,
during, and after a park visit. More than 100 titles are
in print. This is Handbook 110. You may purchase the
handbooks through the mail by writing to the Superintendent of Documents, U.S. Government Printing
Office, Washington, D.C. 20402.

About This Book
Clara Barton National Historic Site in Glen Echo, Mary-
land, a suburb of Washington, D.C., memorializes the
life of Clara Barton, the founder of the American Red
Cross. Part 1 of this book is a chronology of Clara
Barton and her times. Part 2 is a biographical essay.
Part 3 is a guide to the park itself and to National Park
Service and other public and private areas associated
with her career.

Library of Congress Cataloging in Publication Data
United States, National Park Service. Clara Barton,
Clara Barton National Historic Site, Maryland.
(National park handbook; 110) Includes index.

CONTENTS: Clara Barton and her times—Pryor, E.B.
The professional angel—Guide and adviser.
1. Barton, Clara Harlowe, 1821-1912. 2. Clara
Barton National Historic Site, Md.
I. Title. II. Series: United States. National Park
Service. Handbook-National Park Service: 110
HV569.B3U65   1981   361.7'63 [B]   80-607838

Contents

Clara Barton
and Her Times

A Look at the Past

Clara Barton, humanitarian and founder of the American Red Cross, spent the last 15 years of her life in a house in Glen Echo, Maryland, now known as Clara Barton National Historic Site. Here her contributions to American life and her personal achievements are memorialized. Here you can see many of her personal effects and some of the awards given to her. Here, too, you can learn of the substance of her life and see how she lived and worked.

From Glen Echo, you can go on to several other National Park System sites associated with Clara Barton: Antietam, Andersonville, Manassas, Fredericksburg, and Johnstown. Together these diverse sites document her life, her work, and her legacy. Begin here at her house and fill in details of her life as you come across them at the other sites. For example, the lumber you see in the building at Glen Echo was originally used as temporary housing for victims of the Johnstown, Pennsylvania, flood in 1889. After Clara Barton and the Red Cross finished helping the injured and the homeless in that city, the structure was dismantled and shipped to Washington, D.C. Two years later, the materials were used at Glen Echo to construct a national headquarters for the American Red Cross.

The new building had essentially the same lines as the Johnstown structure with various alterations to accommodate the needs of the American Red Cross and Clara Barton herself.

Initially she planned to use this building as a warehouse for American Red Cross supplies. Six years after its construction, the building was remodeled and used not only as

The figures on the preceding two pages are, from left to right: Grand Duchess Louise of Baden, Antoinette Margot, George Kennan, Julian Hubbell, Clara Barton, and Jean-Henri Dunant.

a warehouse, but also as the headquarters of the new organization and as the residence for her and her staff. The structure served all purposes well. Clara Barton did not distinguish between herself and the organization she founded. The lines were blurred; she was the Red Cross, and the Red Cross was Clara Barton. That is evident here in the house, for she did not separate living space from working space. The building's purposes merged in its principal resident.

Using the place as a home, Clara Barton learned to love the passage of the seasons, to enjoy the way the light came in at different times of the year, to plant the yard and garden the way she wanted. As a headquarters and warehouse for the Red Cross, the building served her well, too. She met there with many dignitaries and volunteers on Red Cross business and stored supplies for potential disasters. Her home and office testify to her complete and unequivocal devotion to the Red Cross.

Less sharply focused is Clara Barton's role in women's rights. Miss Barton was neither a traditional woman nor a radical feminist, although Susan B. Anthony and Harriet Austin were friends. She did not repudiate the traditional roles for women. Instead she succeeded in enlarging that accepted sphere so that the traditional skills of women— teaching children, nursing the sick— became acceptable in the public sphere. Clara Barton argued for women's equality and believed in their right to vote. But concern for her fledgling organization overrode her dedication to women's rights and all other causes.

At her home and office in Glen Echo you can begin to sense this complex, fascinating individual: the public and private person so inextricably intertwined. You sense the space in which Clara Barton moved, worked, and thought. Impressions coalesce into an image. And yet that image cannot become distinct without understanding her many ideas, desires, and efforts noted in her diaries, letters, and papers. This handbook tells the story of her eventful 90 years. The next few pages contain a brief chronology of her life and times. Part 2 provides a full-length biographical essay by historian Elizabeth Brown Pryor. Barton in both triumph and defeat is here for the reader to accept, reject, or wonder at. Many of her own words are here to explain more fully what she was thinking—and worrying—about. The biography amplifies the chronology, making it come alive with the whims and inconsistencies of human nature. It's a book within a book. And Part 3 is a guide to sites, managed by the National Park Service and other public and private organizations, associated with Clara Barton and her career.

Together the three parts of this handbook provide a clear image of one of the most outstanding women of the 19th century, Clara Barton.

1821   **Clara Barton is born December 25 in North Oxford, Massachusetts**

1825   John Quincy Adams becomes President; Erie Canal opens

1829   Andrew Jackson becomes President

1830   U.S. population is 12,866,020; Peter Cooper builds first U.S. locomotive

1832   **Clara Barton nurses brother David back to health**; Louisa May Alcott is born

Louisa May Alcott

1834   Cyrus McCormick patents reaper

1835   Sarah and Angelina Grimké become active abolitionists; Samuel Colt patents revolver

Sarah Grimké

Angelina Grimké

1837   Martin Van Buren becomes President

1839   **Clara Barton begins teaching school in North Oxford and continues teaching for the next 11 years;** Mount Holyoke, first college for women, opens

Clara Barton as a schoolteacher

1841   William Henry Harrison becomes President, dies April 4 and is succeeded by John Tyler

1842   Use of anesthetics begins in U.S.

1844   First telegraphic message sent by S.F.B. Morse

1845   James K. Polk becomes President; Margaret Fuller publishes *Woman in the Nineteenth Century;* Frederick Douglass publishes *Narrative of the Life of Frederick Douglass, an American Slave*

1846   Mexican War begins, ends in 1848

1847   American Medical Association is founded

1848   First Women's Rights Convention is held in Seneca Falls, New York

1849	Zachary Taylor becomes President, dies July 9, 1850, and is succeeded by Millard Fillmore; Elizabeth Blackwell becomes first woman to receive M.D. degree

1850 Clara Barton plans to enter Clinton Liberal Institute, Clinton, New York; Harriet Tubman begins helping slaves escape via Underground Railway

Harriet Tubman

1851 Clara Barton's mother dies

1852 Clara Barton starts free school at Bordentown, New Jersey; Harriet Beecher Stowe's *Uncle Tom's Cabin* is published

Harriet Beecher Stowe

1853 Franklin Pierce becomes President; Singer sewing machine factory opens

1854 Clara Barton moves to Washington, D.C., and becomes clerk in Patent Office—at that time the *only* female employed by U.S. Government

1857 Battle of Solferino is fought June 24; James Buchanan becomes President

1859 Edwin Drake drills first oil well

1860 U.S. population is 31,443,321 (includes 3,953,760 slaves and 448,800 free blacks)

1861 Clara Barton begins aid to Union soldiers; Abraham Lincoln becomes President, is assassinated April 15, 1865, and is succeeded by Andrew Johnson; American Civil War begins with firing on Fort Sumter, South Carolina, and ends 1865 at Appomattox Court House, Virginia

Union soldiers near Falmouth, Virginia

Abraham Lincoln

9

1862	Clara Barton's father dies; *Un Souvenir de Solferino* is published by Jean-Henri Dunant
1864	Clara Barton becomes supervisor of nurses for the Army of the James; Treaty of Geneva is signed, thereby establishing the International Red Cross
1865	Clara Barton works at Andersonville, Georgia, to establish national cemetery
1867	U.S. purchases Alaska; first practical typewriter is developed by Christopher Sholes
1868	Andrew Johnson is acquitted in impeachment proceedings; Susan B. Anthony and Elizabeth Cady Stanton begin publication of *The Revolution*

Susan B. Anthony   *Elizabeth Cady Stanton*

1869	Clara Barton begins travels in Europe that last until 1873, and meets Dr. Louis Appia of the International Committee of the Red Cross; U.S. Secretary of State Hamilton Fish rejects Treaty of Geneva; Ulysses S. Grant becomes President; first state board of health is established in Massachusetts

1870 Clara Barton works with Red Cross during Franco-Prussian War, which lasts until 1871

Grand Duchess Louise of Baden

1872	Victoria Woodhull becomes first woman to run for U.S. President
1873	First school of nursing is established at Bellevue Hospital in New York City
1874	Clara Barton meets Julian Hubbell in Dansville, New York; Frances Willard founds Women's Christian Temperance Union; electric streetcars begin running in New York City

Julian Hubbell

1876	Clara Barton collaborates with Susan B. Anthony on biographies of noted women; Alexander Graham Bell invents telephone

1877

Clara Barton begins correspondence with Louis Appia with goal of having U.S. ratify Treaty of Geneva; Rutherford B. Hayes becomes President

Rutherford B. Hayes

1879

Edison invents incandescent light bulb

Drawing from Thomas Edison's notebook, September 1879

1881

Clara Barton founds American Association of the Red Cross, is elected president, establishes first local chapter of the American Red Cross at Dansville, New York, and aids victims of Michigan forest fires; James A. Garfield becomes President, is shot July 2, and is succeeded by Chester Arthur

James A. Garfield   *Chester Arthur*

1882

Clara Barton helps victims of Ohio and Mississippi river floods; U.S. Senate ratifies Treaty of Geneva, March 16, and ratification is proclaimed July 26

Steamboats left high and dry by floodwaters

1883

Clara Barton serves for a short period as superintendent of Women's Reformatory Prison in Sherborn, Massachusetts, and aids victims of tornadoes in Louisiana and Alabama

1884

Clara Barton assists survivors of Ohio and Mississippi river floods; International Red Cross adopts "American Amendment;" study of tuberculosis begins in earnest

1885	Ottmar Mergenthaler invents linotype machine; Grover Cleveland becomes President
1886	**Clara Barton sends relief to Charleston, South Carolina, after earthquake**
1888	**Clara Barton organizes care of Jacksonville, Florida, yellow fever victims**; George Eastman perfects hand camera
1889	**Clara Barton works at Johnstown, Pennsylvania, flood scene**; Benjamin Harrison becomes President; Jane Addams opens Hull House in Chicago; Mayo brothers open clinic in Rochester, Minnesota

Jane Addams

1890	U.S. population stands at 62,947,714
1891	**Clara Barton builds house at Glen Echo, Maryland**

The house at Glen Echo

1892	**Clara Barton organizes relief for victims of drought and famine in Russia**

1893	**Clara Barton sends relief to victims of Sea Island hurricane**; Grover Cleveland becomes President; Lillian Wald establishes Henry Street Settlement House in New York City

Lillian Wald

1895	Röntgen discovers X-rays
1897	**Clara Barton moves to Glen Echo**; William McKinley becomes President, is shot September 6, 1901, dies September 14, and is succeeded by Theodore Roosevelt
1898	**Clara Barton takes the Red Cross to the front lines during Spanish-American War, which lasts from April 11 to August 13, and publishes *The Red Cross in Peace and War***

Red Cross ambulance used during the Spanish-American War

1900   **Clara Barton organizes relief for Galveston, Texas, after hurricane and tidal wave, and receives growing criticism for way she is managing the Red Cross;** Federal charter granted to the American National Red Cross; Walter Reed discovers that mosquitoes transmit yellow fever

1901   Jean-Henri Dunant shares, with Frederic Passy, the first Nobel Peace Prize; Marconi transmits first radio signal across the Atlantic

1902   Arthur Little patents rayon

1903   Wright brothers fly their first airplane

The first flight

1904   **Clara Barton resigns as president of the American National Red Cross;** Mabel Boardman takes control until 1946

Mabel Boardman

1905   **Clara Barton forms the National First Aid Society**

1907   **Clara Barton publishes** *The Story of My Childhood*

At her desk in Glen Echo

1909   William Howard Taft becomes President

1912   **Clara Barton dies April 12 at Glen Echo at age 90**

1915   President Woodrow Wilson lays cornerstone for American National Red Cross headquarters in Washington, D.C.

1963   **Friends of Clara Barton, Inc., purchases house at Glen Echo**

1974   **The U.S. Congress establishes on October 26 Clara Barton National Historic Site**

1975   **National Park Service assumes responsibility for Clara Barton National Historic Site**

The Professional
Angel

Square as a Brick

Sarah Stone Barton was a native New Englander and was born in 1787. She married at age 17, and in her first seven years of marriage, she gave birth to her first four children. The last, Clara, followed after a ten-year interval.

Pages 14 and 15: Clara Barton and Red Cross workers in Tampa, Florida, await transportation to return to Cuba in 1898.

As a woman of 87, Clara Barton remembered "nothing but fear" when she looked back to her childhood. She portrayed herself as an introspective, insecure child, too timid to express her thoughts to others. Yet this girl who felt terror in all new situations possessed the qualities that enabled her to overcome that fear, indeed to become the woman most universally acclaimed as courageous in American history.

Her childhood was unusual. She was born on December 25, 1821, in North Oxford, Massachusetts, and named Clarissa Harlowe Barton after an aunt, who in turn had been named for a popular novel of her day. Her parents, Capt. Stephen Barton and Sarah Stone Barton, had four other children, all at least 10 years of age by the time this child was born. Thus Clara—as she was always called—was born into a world of adults and, as she later recalled, "had no playmates, but in effect six fathers and mothers." She might well have added "six teachers," for she noted that "all took charge of me, all educated me according to personal taste."

Sally Barton, her mother, was an erratic, nervous woman, with a reputation for profanity and a violent temper. She vented her frustrations in compulsive housework, and Clara Barton later recalled that her mother "never slept after 3 o'clock in the morning" and "always did two days work in one." Sally Barton spent little time with her youngest daughter, preferring to leave her with other family members. Thus Clara Barton learned political and military lore from her father, mathematics from her brother Stephen, and horseback riding from brother David. Her two sisters, Sally and Dolly, concentrated on teaching her academic subjects. Besides this household instruction, she attended both private and public schools in the Oxford area.

She was a serious child, anxious to learn, but timid to try. Her later reminiscences of childhood were filled with stories of frightful thunderstorms, intimidating schools, encounters with snakes, and crippling illnesses. When she was six her sister Dolly, who had been an intellectual girl, became mentally unbalanced, and the family had to lock her in a room with barred windows. Once Dolly escaped and chased David's wife, Julia, around the yard with an ax in her hand. Clara Barton never publicly mentioned her sister's insanity, but she privately thought the illness had been brought on by Dolly's unfulfilled desire to obtain a higher education. This rather frantic homelife and the presence of Dolly in the Barton household must have added greatly to her timidity and to her later emotional instability.

Barton developed great loyalty for her family, eccentric as they were. On one occasion she nursed her brother David for two years after he was seriously injured in a fall. Later she used her political influence to assist family members; for example, to defend a cousin's job or to secure suitable military appointment for a relative. Throughout her life she was a faithful correspondent, continually interested in the affairs of nephews, nieces, cousins, brothers, and sisters. And in later years she described her family life in glowing terms, never mentioning her mother's tantrums or Dolly's insanity. Her devotion also extended to family friends.

The Bartons were quintessentially industrious. David and Stephen Barton were businessmen, successful pioneers of milling techniques. Clara Barton's two sisters taught school; a cousin became the first woman Post Office official in Worcester County, Massachusetts. Such diligence was one of the great influences in Clara Barton's life. "You have never known me without work," she wrote when in her eighties, "and you never will. It has always been a part of the best religion I had."

She began work early. She had been an intellectually precocious child and by her late teens was competent to teach. She first taught in the Oxford schools, and later she conducted classes for the children of workers in the Barton family mills. In these one-room schools she gained a reputation for first-rate scholarship and excellent discipline. She expelled and whipped students when necessary, but mostly she cajoled them into obedience through affection and respect. When her first school won the district's highest marks for discipline, she remonstrated: "I thought it the greatest injustice . . . [for] there had been no discipline. . . . Child that I was, I did not know that the surest test of discipline is its absence."

Barton was introspective and keenly aware of herself as an individual, and this enabled her to view her students individually. She gave them such personal attention that scores of former pupils wrote to her in later years, confident that their uniqueness had touched her. Barton in turn called her pupils "my boys" and made no apologies for her loyalty. "They were all mine," she recalled in the second part of her autobiography, "second only to the claims and interests of the real mother. . . . And so they had remained. Scattered over the world, some near, some far, I have been their confidant. . . . I count little in comparison with the faithful grateful love I hold today of the few survivors of my Oxford school."

Teaching thus reinfored her loyalty and her sense of individuality. Her excellence as an instructor also had the effect of mitigating her introversion and strengthening her self-assurance. Indeed, she became confident enough to teach the roughest district schools and to demand pay equal to a man's. " I may sometimes be willing to teach for nothing," she told one school board, "but if paid at all, I shall never do a man's work for less than a man's pay."

In 1850, after more than ten years of successful teaching, she felt compelled to "find a school . . . to teach *me* something." Female academies were rare. She settled upon the Clinton Liberal Institute in Clinton, New York, and took as many classes as possible in her course.

The institute was, in many ways, an ideal academy for Barton. The school's liberal philosophy and broad approach to education for women corresponded with her family's liberal traditions and her own political and religious feelings. Moreover, the climate of New England and New York in the 1830s and 1840s was one of intellectual and moral progressiveness: Horace Mann instituted far-reaching educational reforms in Massachusetts; Ralph Waldo Emerson wrote about the philosophic basis of human liberty; religion lost its evangelistic approach; William Lloyd Garrison expounded on the plight of the enslaved black; and a few women such as Elizabeth Cady Stanton realized that their position was little better than that of slaves and protested against it.

None of this activity was lost on Clara Barton, who possessed an innate sense of honesty and justice. She became an early advocate of rights for women. "I must have been born believing," she wrote, "in the full right of woman to all the privileges and positions which nature and justice accord her in common with other human beings. Perfectly equal rights—human rights. There was never any question in my mind in regard to this." She supported the cause of woman suffrage, for she maintained that while a woman was denied the vote she "had no rights and . . . must submit to wrongs, and because she submits to wrongs she isn't anybody." Yet she steadfastly asserted her rights and deemed it "ridiculous that any sensible, rational person should question it." Although she did not participate in women's rights rallies until later in her life, she always acted on her principles. In February 1861, for example, Barton began to champion the cause of her cousin, Elvira Stone, a postmistress who was about to lose her job to a man. Barton laid the unpleasant facts before her friends in Washington without hesitation: "As Cousin Elvira had never taken any parts [*sic*] in politics . . . political tendencies can scarcely be made a pretext, neither incompetence, neglect of business, location or lack of a proper recognition of, or attention to, the wants of the community in any manner—And it would not *look well* to commence a petition with *Mankind* being naturally prone to selfishness we hereby etc., etc.—And I have

Stephen Barton was a descen-
dant of Edward Barton who had
come to Salem, Massachusetts,
in 1640. Stephen, born in 1774,
served in the Indian Wars in
Ohio Territory during the 1790s
under Mad Anthony Wayne.

David Barton was a keen horse-
man. In later years Clara
Barton referred to him as the
"Buffalo Bill of the neighbor-
hood" when recalling the
events of her childhood. David
and his brother Stephen owned
and operated a satinet mill;
satinet was a kind of cotton
cloth.

19

been able to divine nothing except that she is guilty of being a woman." By April she had secured her cousin's position. She dryly remarked that Elvira Stone was certainly entitled to it, for, "I have never learned that the [post office] proceeds arising from the female portion of the correspondence of our country were deducted from the revenue."

Barton felt that by winning such small battles, her larger feminist principles were upheld. But her real contribution in these early years was her own attitude and actions. By demonstrating that her talents, courage, and intellect were undeniably equal to a man's she quietly furthered the women's cause as much as parades and speeches did. "As for my being a woman," she told the men who questioned her, [you] will get used to that."

Her interest in the extension of liberties for women was not selfishly inspired. Rather it was a product of her deep-rooted sense of integrity and fairness. She believed rigidly in human rights, especially in the rights of those unable to defend or help themselves. "What is everybody's business is nobody's business," Barton once declared. "What is nobody's business is my business." Her advocacy of equality colored her political views.

Neither could Barton tolerate dishonesty and petty arrogance. More than once during the Civil War she railed against "the conduct of improper, heartless, unfaithful Union officers" who blithely ignored the plight of the "dirty, lousy, common soldiers." She expected high standards of politicians, soldiers, and schoolboys alike. Once when a former pupil had misused some money she had entrusted to him, she lamented: "I am less grieved by the loss than I am about his manner of treating my trust. . . . I am as square as a brick and I expect my boys to be square."

In 1852, Barton demonstrated the sincerity of her principles in a dramatic way. She left Clinton to stay with a schoolmate near Bordentown, New Jersey, and taught at a private subscription school, for there were no free public schools. She felt uneasy about the numbers of children whose parents could not afford private instruction, and she began to agitate for a free school. But the popular view was that free schools were a form of charity. She refused to give in and eventually swayed the local school board. A small house was outfitted, and she began to lead one of the first free schools in the state.

The Bordentown free school was a pronounced success. In its first year the number of pupils rose from 6 to 600, and the town built a new schoolhouse. The town, however, could not accept a woman as the head of a school of 600 pupils and a man was named principal. She became his assistant. "I could bear the ingratitude, but not the pettiness and jealousy of this principal."

Whether the pettiness was real or imagined, Barton could not endure a secondary position. While she debated resignation, her nerves gave way, causing a case of laryngitis. Early in 1854, she resigned and left for Washington, D.C., where she hoped to improve her health and "do something decided" with her newly realized "courage and tolerable faculty of winning [her] way with strangers."

Barton's health did improve in

James Buchanan (1791-1869) held several public offices before becoming President in 1857. He was a member of the Pennsylvania House of Representatives and of the U.S. House of Representatives and Senate. He was secretary of state for James K. Polk and ambassador to Great Britian during the Presidency of Franklin Pierce. As President he felt powerless to deal with the States that seceded in the last months of his administration though he abhorred their actions. He retired to his home in Lancaster, Pennsylvania.

Washington, and she was soon able to "do something decided." Charles Mason, the commissioner of patents, hired her as a clerk. At this time no women were permanently employed by the Federal Government though previously there had been. Most officials agreed with Secretary of the Interior Robert McClelland who declared that there was an "obvious impropriety in the mixing of the two sexes within the walls of a public office." She gained the confidence of Commissioner Mason, however, and became his most competent and trusted clerk. Moreover, she combatted the many dishonest clerks who sold patent privileges illegally. The whole affair, she concluded, made quite a commotion, and the clerks "tried to make it too hard for me. It wasn't a very pleasant experience; in fact it was very trying, but I thought perhaps there was some question of principle involved and I lived through it."

Although she lost her job at the Patent Office under the Buchanan administration in 1856, Barton was reappointed late in 1860. She enjoyed living in Washington, for she was fascinated by politics and liked knowing such prominent figures as Massachusetts Senator Henry Wilson. She often sat in the Senate gallery to watch the proceedings and became astute and well-informed on political matters.

Clara Barton was still a clerk at the Patent Office when the Civil War began. Like many other intelligent and independent women of her day, she was often filled with restless discontent, probably stemming from having more to give than life demanded. Her job as Patent Office clerk demanded little but self-efface-

21

ment and neat penmanship. The conflict that arose in 1861 provided her with an outlet for her energy and satisfied her longing to lose herself in her work and to be needed.

Doing Something Decided

When President Lincoln issued his call for volunteers to maintain the Union, the response was immediate and troops began heading for Washington. Some Massachusetts volunteers passing through Baltimore, which was decidedly Southern in sentiment, were attacked by local citizens.

In late April 1861, less than two weeks after the bombardment of Fort Sumter in South Carolina, the Massachussetts Sixth Regiment arrived in Washington, D.C., from Massachusetts. This regiment hailed from the Worcester area and many of the men were friends or former pupils of Clara Barton. Their train was mobbed while passing through Baltimore, and Barton, concerned that one of her "boys" might have been injured, rushed to their temporary quarters in the Senate Chamber. She found the Regiment unharmed, but sadly lacking in basic necessities— "towels and handkerchiefs . . . serving utensils, thread, needles . . . etc." She bought and distributed as many of these items as she could, then wrote to the anxious families in Massachusetts to send preserved fruits, blankets, candles, and other supplies to supplement the unreliable army issues. "It is *said* upon proper authority, that 'our army is supplied,' " she wrote to a group of ladies in Worcester, "how this can be so I fail to see." When the generous New Englanders inundated her with useful articles and stores, Barton's home became a virtual warehouse. "It may be in these days of quiet idleness they have really no pressing wants," she observed, "but in the event of a battle who can tell what their needs might grow to in a single day?" Such garnering of supplies against unforeseen disaster eventually became a central characteristic of her relief work in the years to come.

Barton's earliest concern with aiding the Union army stemmed from her loyalty to the Massachusetts men. She felt a personal involvement with those who "only a few years ago came every morning . . . and took their places quietly and happily among my scholars" and an allegiance to others from her home state. "They formed and crowded around me," she noted. "What could I do but go with them, or work for them and my country? The patriot blood of my father was warm in my veins."

Her patriotism also was aroused by the Union cause. Although she maintained that the purpose of the war was not solely to abolish slavery, she also held little sympathy for the Southern way of life and aligned herself with such Republicans as Henry Wilson who believed that historically the Southern states had conspired to tyrannize the North. "Independence!" she once scoffed, "they always had their independence till they madly threw it away." She was exhilarated. "This conflict is one thing I've been waiting for," she told a friend, "I'm well and strong and young—young enough to go to the front. If I can't be a soldier I'll help soldiers." And feeling even more exalted, she declared that "when there is no longer a soldier's arm to raise the Stars and Stripes above our Capitol, may God give strength to mine."

For a year Barton contented herself with soliciting supplies. Then, as the horrible effects of battle were reported in Washington, she began to think of aiding soldiers directly on the battlefield. She had visited hospitals and invalid camps, but what disturbed her most were the tales of suffering at the front. Soldiers often had wounds unnecessarily complicated by infection due to neglect, or died of thirst while waiting for transportation to field hospitals. Nurses were urgently needed at the battlefield, but she wondered if it was seemly for a woman to place herself directly in the lines of battle: "I struggled . . . with my sense of propriety, with the appalling fact that I was only a woman whispering in one ear, and thundering in the other [were] the groans of suffering men dying like dogs."

Her father encouraged her to go where her conscience directed. When Captain Barton died in March 1862, she felt that her duties to the family had closed. She petitioned Massachusetts Gov. John Andrew and other government officials for permission to join General Burnside's division at the front. Late in the summer of 1862, at the Battle of Cedar Mountain, Virginia, she "broke the shackles and went to the field."

At Cedar Mountain, and the subsequent second battle of Bull Run, she began a remarkable service which continued to the end of the war. Here, for the first of many times, Barton and her "precious freights" were transported in railroad cars or by heavy, jolting army wagons to a scene of utter desolation and confusion. When she arrived at Bull Run, 3,000 wounded men were lying in a sparsely wooded field on straw, for there was no other bedding. Most had not eaten all day; many faced amputations or other operations. She was unprepared for such carnage, but she distributed coffee, crackers, and the few other supplies she had brought. With calico skirt pinned up around her waist, she moved among

Andersonville prison camp in Georgia

Confederate dead at Antietam

the men and prayed that the combination of lighted candles and dry straw would not result in a fire that would engulf them.

Scanty as her supplies were, Barton's aid was timely and competent. An army surgeon, Dr. James I. Dunn, wrote to his wife: "At a time when we were entirely out of dressings of every kind, she supplied us with everything, and while the shells were bursting in every direction . . . she staid [sic] dealing out shirts . . . and preparing soup and seeing it prepared in all the hospitals. . . . I thought that night if heaven ever sent out a homely angel, she must be one, her assistance was so timely."

Dunn's letter was widely published during the Civil War, and he was embarrassed that his private portrayal of Barton as a "homely angel" ever saw print. She, too, seems to have been embarrassed, for she crossed the word out on the newspaper clippings she kept and substituted the word "holy" for "homely." Although the original letter shows that Dunn did indeed mean "homely," Barton's biographers have taken their cue from her and given her the title "the holy angel."

These early battles taught Clara Barton how poorly prepared the Union army was for the immense slaughter taking place and how immediate battlefield aid meant much more than a battalion of nurses back in Washington.

In quick succession the battles of Fairfax Court House and Chantilly followed second Bull Run. A surgeon recalled that at Chantilly "we had nothing but our instruments— not even a bottle of wine. When the [railroad] cars whistled up to the station, the first person on the platform was Miss Barton again to supply us with . . . every article that could be thought of. She staid [sic] there till the last wounded soldier was placed on the cars." She worked for five days in the pouring rain with only two hours of sleep. As at all battles, she took time to jot down the names of many wounded men, so that their families could be informed.

Barely two weeks later, on September 14, she again went to the field, this time with advance information about a battle to be fought near Harpers Ferry, Virginia (now West Virginia). She arrived too late but rushed on to Antietam, which she reached at the height of battle on September 17. Once again, she cooked gruel, braved enemy fire to feed the wounded, and provided surgeons with precious medical supplies. She had a narrow escape from death when a bullet passed under her arm, through the sleeve of her dress, and killed the wounded soldier cradled in her arms.

In all this fury, Barton was unflappable. At the Battle of Fredericksburg in December 1862, "a shell destroyed the door of the room in which she was attending to wounded men," recalled co-worker Rev. C.M. Welles. "She did not flinch, but continued her duties as usual." And she was working at the Lacy House, where hundreds of men were crowded into 12 rooms, when a courier rushed up the steps and placed a crumpled, bloody slip of paper in her hands. It was a request from a surgeon asking her to cross the Rappahannock River to Fredericksburg where she was urgently needed. As always, hospital space was inadequate, and dying men, lying in the December chill, were freezing to the ground. With shells and bullets whistling around her, Barton bravely crossed the swaying pontoon bridge. As she reached the end of the bridge an officer stepped to her side to help her down. "While our hands were raised, a piece of an exploding shell hissed through between us, just below our arms, carrying away a portion of both the skirts of his coat and my dress." She made her way into Fredericksburg without further mishap. She was lucky; the gallant officer who helped her on the bridge was brought to her a half hour later—dead.

Bravery and timeliness were conspicuous elements of Barton's Civil War service. But of equal importance was her compassion for the individual soldier. And she treated the wounded of both sides alike. Her relief work was also notable for its resourcefulness. She built fires, extracted bullets with a pocket knife, made gallons of applesauce, baked pies "with crinkly edges," drove teams, and performed last rites. When all other food gave out she concocted a mixture of wine, whiskey, sugar, and army biscuit crumbs. "Not very inviting," she admitted, "but always acceptable." When she lacked serving implements, she emptied jars of fruit and jelly and used them. When tired she propped herself against a tent pole or slept sitting up in a wagon. The common soldier remembered her sympathy and tenderness, the officer her calmness and alert activity under fire.

As historian R. H. Bremer notes, Barton viewed her role in the war as something of a family matter. If she was a "ministering angel," she was also "everybody's old-maid aunt"— fussing over "my boys," worrying over clothes and food, and treating the men as fond nephews. Much of her success with quartermasters, officers, and men was due to this attitude, which eclipsed suspicion of her as a woman and radiated the sentimentality of the time.

She pursued her self-appointed task with remarkable tenacity. Her contribution was unique, for she worked directly on the battlefield, not behind the lines in a hospital. She worked primarily alone—and liked it that way. Although she respected such organizations as the Sanitary Commission, she felt that by working independently she could comfortably assist where she saw need. She wanted to be her own boss and be appreciated for her individual efforts. She did not seek glory, but she needed praise and did not wish to have it bestowed on the name of an impersonal group or commission.

There is no question that Clara Barton hugely enjoyed acclaim. She liked being in the inner elite of wartime politics, for it gave her the chance to shine as a personality, to be revered as an "Angel of the Battlefield." In later life she enjoyed trips to Europe that amounted to triumphal tours.

Barton's relief work benefitted her in another way. Throughout her life she was self-conscious and introspective, preoccupied with small personal incidents which she magnified out of proportion to their importance. She once described herself as "like other people . . . only sometimes a 'little more so,' " and the description is apt. She was inwardly pessimistic, and highly sensitive to criticism. She confided to her diary that she felt "pursued by a shadow" and spent years with

Continues on page 30

Clara Barton was not the only civilian who ministered to the wounded during the Civil War. The nature of this conflict was so personal and so immediate that many hundreds of volunteers gave enormously of their time in hospitals and on the field. In the North, Dorothea Dix interrupted her pre-war work with the insane to become superintendent of Female Nurses; Walt Whitman, Louisa May Alcott, Frances Dana Gage, and "Mother" Mary Ann Bickerdyke are a few of the other famous names connected with such service. Of especial importance were the Christian and Sanitary Commissions, organizations which worked with the government in camp and on the battlefield to improve the lot of the Union soldier. In the Confederacy, stringent financial conditions and widely scattered population prevented relief efforts from being as organized as those of the North. But charity had a deep-rooted meaning for the Southern cause, and self-denial became a matter of pride. "We had no Sanitary Commission in the South," wrote one Confederate veteran, "we were too poor. . . . With us each house was a hospital."

The United States Sanitary Commission was established in April 1861. It was originally designed for inquiry into the health of the troops and as an advisory board to the government on improvement of sanitary conditions in the army. In the early months of the war, the Sanitary Commission attempted to methodize the fragmented benevolent efforts of the Union. It fought favoritism to particular regiments with equitable distribution of supplies, administered from a network of regional and local auxiliaries. By 1863, however, the commission was, of necessity, drawn to the battlefield, where it established hospital and transport ships, supply stations, and gave direct aid to the wounded. Several million dollars were raised by the commission through "Sanitary Fairs," large fund-raising bazaars. At one point the Sanitary Commission had more than 500 agents working in the field. By its impartiality and organization, the Sanitary Commission was the forerunner of the Red Cross in concept, if not in actuality.

Another organization, drawn along similar lines, was the United States Christian Commission. Established by a group of New York churches in 1862, its object was to "give relief and sympathy and then the Gospel." Volunteers in the Christian Commission were called "Ambassadors of Jesus;" they were chosen

Dorothea Dix (1802-87) started teaching Sunday School at the East Cambridge House of Corrections in Massachusetts in 1841. The appalling conditions she observed there spurred her to attempt to reform prisons and mental institutions. This work preoccupied her the rest of her life. She died in Trenton, New Jersey.

*From Clara Barton's poem,
"The Women Who Went to the Field."

"They would stand with you now, as they stood with you then,
The nurses, consolers and saviors of men." *The Women Who Went to the Field*

largely from the ranks of clergymen and YMCA members but many women were among its workers. The Christian Commission did give battlefield relief, and sought to supply reading material, clothing, and medicine.

Clara Barton was familiar with these organizations, and, especially in the latter part of the war, often worked alongside them. But though she wrote publicly that their labor was always in "perfect accord, mutual respect and friendliness," she chose to work alone rather than align herself too closely with the commissions. Barton's natural leadership and difficulty in working with others prompted her to remain independent, where she would not be "compromised by them in the least." Furthermore, she secretly scorned the commissions' work, which she thought inexperienced and impractical: "an old fudge" she called the Sanitary Commission in her journal.

Mary Ann Bickerdyke

Barton also chose not to work with Dorothea Dix's "Department of Female Nurses." A compulsive humanitarian worker, Dix had volunteered her services to the War Department at the opening of hostilities. Her offer was accepted and Dix began the impossible task of collecting supplies, selecting nurses, and supervising hospitals for the Union army. Dix was a perfectionist and her dogmatic and strident opinions won her few friends. But her sharp altercations with physicians and officers resulted more from frustration because she could not relieve the massive misery, than from an over-bearing personality. Feeling that she had failed to achieve her mission, Dix wrote at war's end: "This is not the work I would have my life judged by."

The use of female nurses was an innovation during the Civil War and Dix was anxious for the women under her to be taken seriously. Fearful that nursing would become a sport among adventurous young women, she laid down stringent and inflexible rules for nurses. These rules would have greatly hampered Clara Barton's independent spirit and this is one reason she chose not to join Dix's force.

In addition to the official organizations there were numerous "unsung heroes" during the Civil War. Most notable were the religious orders such as the Sisters of Charity who calmly defied the army's restrictions and worked both at the front and in hospitals. Despite the fact that such diverse groups inevitably caused conflicts and jealousies, the Civil War provided a field large enough for all of the humanitarian organizations which labored in it.

Walt Whitman

"scarcely one cheerful day." Periodically she became so depressed that she could not "see much these days worth living for; cannot but think it will be a quiet resting place when all these cares and vexations and anxieties are over, and I no longer give or take offense. I . . . have grown weary of life at an age when other people are enjoying it most."

While aiding others, Barton, for a time, forgot herself. Her "work and words," she insisted, were solely bound up in "the individual soldier—what he does, sees, feels, or thinks in . . . long dread hours of leaden rain and iron hail." As she gained self-confidence and acclaim, she shed her morbid introspection. Once when she was asked if her work had been interesting, she gave a revealing reply: "When you stand day and night in the presence of hardship and physical suffering, you do not stop to think about the interest. There is no time for that. Ease pain, soothe sorrow, lessen suffering—this is your only thought day and night. Everything, everything else is lost sight of—yourself and the world."

In April 1863, Barton transferred her base from Washington to Hilton Head Island off the coast of South Carolina. She had been advised that a major siege of Charleston would be attempted and believed she could be most useful there. She also hoped to be closer to her brothers: Stephen lived behind Confederate lines in North Carolina, and David had been sent by the army to Hilton Head in the early days of 1863.

During the eight-month siege of Charleston, she worked on the battlefields of Morris Island and Fort Wagner and helped nurse soldiers dying of malaria and other tropical fevers. Charleston proved to be a less active spot than anticipated, however, and this fact, coupled with a growing rift between Barton and hospital authorities, led her to leave the area in January 1864. She returned to Washington, where she continued to gather supplies as she awaited her next chance for service.

Her chance came in May 1864, when "the terrible slaughter of the Wilderness and Spotsylvania turned all pitying hearts once more to Fredericksburg." Here she witnessed some of the most frightening scenes she ever encountered. Fifty thousand men were killed or wounded in the Wilderness Campaign. "I saw many things that I did not wish to see and I pray God I may never see again," she told a friend. Rain turned the red clay soil of Virginia to deep mud, and hundreds of army wagons, crowded full of wounded and suffering men, were stuck in a tremendous traffic jam. "No hub of a wheel was in sight and you saw nothing of any animal below its knees."

She immediately set about feeding the men in the stalled wagons, but another, more appalling situation arose. Some "heartless, unfaithful officers" decided that it was, in fact, a hardship on the refined citizens of Fredericksburg to be compelled to open their homes as hospitals for "these dirty, lousy, common soldiers." Always a champion of the "army blue" against the "gold braid," she hurried to Washington to advise her friend Henry Wilson of the predicament. Wilson, chairman of the Senate Military Affairs Committee, swiftly warned the War Department. One day later the homes of Fredericksburg were opened to Union soldiers. She returned to the battlefield with additional supplies and continued to help the wounded. "When I rose, I wrung the blood from the bottom of my clothing before I could step, for the weight about my feet."

After the Wilderness Campaign she served as a supervisor of nurses for the Army of the James, under Gen. Benjamin F. Butler, until January 1865. She organized hospitals and nurses and administered day-to-day activities in the invalid camps that received the wounded from Cold Harbor, Petersburg, and other battles near Richmond. Many of these soldiers remembered her thoughtfulness. If a wounded man requested codfish cakes "in the old home way," he most likely got them; a young soldier, wasted to a skeleton, was tenderly cared for until his relatives arrived to take him home; requests to have letters written were never too much trouble.

At the end of the Civil War an exhausted Clara Barton felt certain of one thing: "I have labored up to the full measure of my strength." And she labored without pay and often used her own funds to buy supplies. In the field she shared the conditions of the common soldier: "I have always refused a tent unless the army had tents also, and I have never eaten a mouthful . . . until the sick of the army were abundantly supplied." Her pragmatic judgment and ability to work under the most dangerous and awkward of conditions earned her the respect of surgeons and generals who ordinarily considered they had "men enough to act as nurses" and did not want women around to "skeddadle and create a panic." General Butler described her as having "executive ability and kind-

Throughout the Civil War Benjamin Butler (1818-93) was a controversial figure as he invariably was at odds with the national administration on the treatment of the civilian population and the black slaves. Leaving the Army, he went into politics and served in the U.S. Congress and one term as governor of Massachusetts. It was as governor that he appointed Clara Barton superintendent of the Women's Reformatory at Sherborn.

Frederick Douglass (1817?-95) was born in Talbot County, Maryland, the son of a white man and a slave woman. He was an eloquent spokesman for American blacks before and after the Civil War and spent his life fighting for equality. He was appointed U.S. minister to Haiti in 1889.

heartedness, with an honest love of the work of reformation and care of her living fellow creatures."

Barton's perceptive and sympathetic nature led her to foresee innumerable social problems after the Civil War. A champion of the underdog, she was concerned with the precarious situation of the newly freed slaves. What she saw on her travels to the South was alarming: uneducated, dependent blacks were being duped by their former masters, and freedom was, in many cases, a burden, not a blessing. Few blacks knew of the laws passed for their benefit and many did not understand that they must continue to work. She observed that the former "owners were disposed to cheat [a] great many." Wherever she went, Barton tried to explain the law and the meaning of freedom to the blacks, many of whom walked great distances to ask her advice.

Barton, however, did more than advise. She consulted with Senator Wilson about the best possible personnel for the Freedman's Bureau and lobbied Congress for a bill allowing blacks to use surplus army goods. She attended meetings of the Freedman's Aid Society and sent reports on blacks' conditions to the Freedman's Bureau. She also worked for the extension of suffrage through "Universal Franchise" meetings and the American Equal Rights Association; she spoke at their rallies and formed lifelong attachments with such prominent leaders as Frederick Douglass and Anna Dickenson. During October of 1868, she began to formulate a plan for helping "the colored sufferers." The plan, modelled on the work of Josephine Griffing, apparently involved the use of abandoned barracks and former hospitals near Washington for "Industrial Houses." Here Freedmen could learn a trade and be "provided with the means of self-support and so command the respect of [their] former masters." She discussed her ideas with several people, but unfortunately, the project was dropped because of her failing health.

Barton remained a staunch ally of blacks during her lifetime. Blacks employed by her received wages consistent with those of whites and generally received additional training and education. When few other charitable groups were willing to aid blacks who were the victims of natural disasters, such as the storm that hit the Sea Islands of South Carolina in 1893, Barton's Red Cross never hesitated. And those who denied the bravery or competence of black troops in the Civil or Spanish-American Wars found her an outspoken opponent. Made honorary president of a society honoring soldiers of the Spanish-American War, she resigned when she found that it was open only to whites.

At the same time she was promoting the enfranchisement of freedmen, she embarked on a project aimed at diminishing another major post-war problem: the whereabouts of thousands of missing soldiers. She appreciated the difficulty of keeping accurate records in the confusion of battle and understood that it was often nearly impossible to recognize the dead, or identify individual graves among the hastily dug common trenches. Her wartime notebooks and diaries are filled with names of missing and wounded soldiers and lists of those who died in her arms with perhaps no one else to know their fate. With official permission from President Lincoln, she devised a plan to identify missing soldiers by publishing in newspapers monthly rolls of men whose families or friends had inquired. Any person with information could write to her and she would forward it to those concerned.

As she went about her work she learned that not everyone was willing to be found. Soldiers who were attached to Southern sweethearts, who had deserted, or who simply wished to start a new life, preferred to remain missing. One young man wanted to know what he had done to have his name "blazoned all over the country" in newspapers. "What you have done . . . I certainly *do not* know," she replied. "It seems to have been the misfortune of your family to think more of you than you did of them, and probably more than you deserve from the manner in which you treat them. . . . I shall inform them of your existence lest you should not 'see fit' to do so yourself."

In all, Barton's "Office of Correspondence with Friends of the Missing Men of the United States Army" worked for four years to bring information to more than 22,000 families. The most help she received came from a young man named Dorence Atwater, a former Andersonville prisoner. He fortuitously had copied the names of more than 13,000 men who had died during his confinement. With his aid, she identified all but 400 of the Andersonville graves and caused the camp to be made a National Cemetery.

Atwater's help was invaluable, and he became a close personal friend. She was highly indignant when the

Federal Government arrested Atwater on charges that his death list was government property. Federal officials claimed that he had "stolen" back the list after turning it over to the War Department. The case appears to have been actually based on confusion and a stubborn refusal of both sides to back down, but Clara Barton was incensed. She fought for Atwater's release with every influential person she knew; she advised and prompted his statements from prison and carried on a monumental publicity campaign to elicit public sympathy. Largely because of her efforts, he was freed.

Atwater's defense and her work with the missing men further developed her publicity efforts, which she had used so effectively in the Civil War. As time went on, her relief work relied more and more on public support. "We enter a field of distress," she wrote, "study conditions, learn its needs, and state these facts calmly, and truthfully to the people of the entire country through all its channels of information and leave them free to use their own judgments in regard to the assistance they will render." Still, she knew how to publicize her causes dramatically. In 1886, when a tornado struck Mount Vernon, Illinois, she wrote: "the pitiless snow is falling on the heads of 3,000 people who are without homes, without food, or clothing." The response was immediate.

Oral publicity also proved helpful during her attempt to identify missing men. In 1866, she began a successful lecture tour that publicized both her cause and her name. She gave lectures throughout the North and West and was featured on tours with such prominent speakers as Ralph Waldo Emerson, William Lloyd Garrison, and Mark Twain. Her talks centered on "Work and Incidents of Army Life." The flyer portrayed her lectures as "exquisitely touching and deeply interesting, frequently moving her audience to tears." As always, she enjoyed the notoriety and in her diary wrote a flattering description of herself at the lecturn: "easy and graceful, neith[er] tall nor short, neith[er] large nor small . . . head large and finely shaped with a profusion of jet-black hair . . . with no manner of ornament save its own glossy beauty. . . . She [is] *well* dressed. . . . Her voice . . . at first low and sweet but falling upon the ear with a clearness of tone and distinctness of utterance at once surprising and entrancing."

Although she enjoyed being in the limelight, many of her old insecurities returned. "All speech-making terrifies me," she said, "first I have no taste for it, lastly I hate it." In 1868, while delivering a lecture in Boston, she suffered what was apparently a nervous breakdown and was ordered by her doctors to recuperate in Europe.

The periodic nervous disorders she suffered appear to have been directly related to her sense of usefulness. When she was not working, her diary entries often begin "Have been sad all day," or "This was one of the most down-spirited days that ever comes to me." She once remarked that nothing made her so sick of life as to feel she was wasting it. As long as she was needed, admired, demanded, she could perform near miracles of self-denial and courageous action. When the crisis ebbed, she became despondent and sick, requiring attention of a different sort. As a single woman, often removed from her family, she had no other way to attract notice than to excel as an individual. When such an opportunity faded, or when she found herself an object of criticism, she was, in several senses, prostrated. When her interest was again aroused by the chance of giving service, her health and spirits rebounded.

Battling for Ratification

Jean-Henri Dunant

Clara Barton arrived in Great Britain in late August 1869 with no definite plans. Her doctors had ordered rest and a change of scene. She toured London, visited Paris, then proceeded to Geneva. She thought she might stay in Switzerland, but the depressing fall weather changed her mind; she moved to Corsica, seeking sun and wishing to visit the haunts of her longtime hero, Napoleon I.

She was ill, edgy, and demanding. Corsica, although beautiful, did not suit her and by March she was back in Geneva. Here, by chance, she was introduced to Dr. Louis Appia, a member of the International Committee of the Red Cross. This organization was the result of the Geneva Convention of 1864, which produced a treaty dealing with the treatment of wounded and sick soldiers, prisoners of war, and civilians under wartime conditions. The convention was inspired by a book entitled *Un Souvenir de Solferino* (A Memory of Solferino), in which author Jean-Henri Dunant described the horrors of the Battle of Solferino. At the time of her meeting with Appia, she had not heard of the Geneva Convention nor of Dunant. When she finally read Dunant's work, she must have identified strongly with it, for he expressed perfectly the concern for the individual which had prompted Barton's Civil War aid: "A son idolized by his parents, brought up and cherished for years by a loving mother who trembled with alarm over his slightest ailment; a brilliant officer beloved by his family, with wife and children at home; a young soldier who had left sweetheart or mother, sisters or old father to go to war; all lie stretched in the mud and dust, drenched in their own blood."

At their first meeting, Appia asked Barton why the United States had not signed the Treaty of Geneva. A U.S. delegate, Charles Bowles, had been at the Geneva Convention, and Dr. Henry Bellows, president of the Sanitary Commission, had urged the government to accede to the treaty. But the United States remained the only major nation that had not accepted the international pact. Barton said a key factor was probably the American public's almost total ignorance about the treaty, and she asked Appia to provide her with further information about the International Red Cross.

Barton soon found reason, in her words, "to respect the cause and appreciate the work of the Geneva Convention." On July 19, 1870, France declared war on Prussia. She was restless and excited by hearing guns at practice and wrote to Appia, offering her services to the Red Cross. Before he could reply, however, she made her way to Basel, Switzerland, where she worked with Red Cross volunteers making bandages. This tame work exasperated her. "It is not like me, nor like my past to be sitting quietly where I can just watch the sky reddening with the fires of a bombarded city and . . . have [nothing] to do with it." De-

spite her frustration, Barton's work in Basel gave her great respect for the garnering power of the Red Cross. Its warehouses were stocked with supplies of all kinds, and trained nurses and clerks wearing Red Cross armbands stood ready to assist. "I . . . saw the work of these Red Cross societies in the field, accomplishing in four months under this systematic organization what we failed to accomplish in four years without it—no mistakes, no needless suffering, no starving, no lack of care, no waste, no confusion, but order, plenty, cleanliness, and comfort wherever that little flag made its way, a whole continent marshalled under the banner of the Red Cross—as I saw all this, and joined and worked in it, you will not wonder that I said to myself, 'If I live to return to my country, I will try to make my people understand the Red Cross and that treaty.' "

The opportunity to be useful and to forget petty irritants restored her health. "I am so glad to be able to work once more," she told her cousin, Elvira Stone, "I *have* worked . . . all year, and grown stronger and better." She then made her way toward the battlefields of France accompanied by Antoinette Margot, a young Swiss woman. On their way toward Mulhouse, where several battles had been reported, they met hundreds of refugees who pleaded with them to turn back. But when they encountered trouble from German troops, Barton brought out a sewing kit and speedily tacked a cross of red ribbon onto the sleeve of her dress. Thus began her first service under the Red Cross badge, which she would wear long and proudly.

Napoleon III, Emperor of France

Otto von Bismarck, Chancellor of Germany

Wilhelm I, Emperor of Germany

Barton was disappointed to learn that she was not needed at the front, but she found her niche elsewhere. As she traveled through France, she wrote to newspaper editor Horace Greeley that she had seen deserted fields, "crops spoiled . . . by both friend and foe. Her producing population stands under arms or wasting in prisons—her hungry cattle slain for food or rotting of disease—her homes deserted or smouldering in ashes." When Louise, grand duchess of Baden and a Red Cross patron, asked her to help establish hospitals and distribute clothing to destitute civilians, she undertook the work with zeal.

Barton's accomplishments during the Franco-Prussian War lay mainly in aid to civilians. Her most notable work was in Strasbourg, where she used her powers of organization and publicity to establish a sewing center to clothe the city's destitute population. In a letter to a generous English philanthropist in May 1871, she wrote: "Thousands who are well today will rot with smallpox and be devoured by body-lice before the end of August. Against . . . these two scourges there is, I believe, no check but the destruction of all infected garments; hence the imperative necessity for something to take their place. Excuse, sir, I pray you, the plain ugly terms which I have employed to express myself; the facts are plain and ugly."

Barton did not confine her activity to Strasbourg. After eight months work, she left her sewing establishment in the hands of local officials and journeyed to Paris where she distributed clothing, money, and comfort to citizens. From Paris she went to Lyons and surveyed the sur-

Continues on page 40

37

Jean-Henri Dunant and the Geneva Convention

On June 24, 1859, forces commanded by French Emperor Napoleon III and Austria's Emperor Franz Josef, met on the battlefield of Solferino, in Northern Italy. More than 40,000 men were killed or wounded in the battle, and towns and villages throughout the area became temporary, crude hospitals. In nearby Castiglione, a stranger, dressed in white, watched with horror as dazed and suffering soldiers were slowly brought from the battlefield only to be met with a shortage of doctors, inadequate accommodations, and an appalling lack of food and supplies. With spirit and speed "the man in white" began to recruit local peasants for volunteer service and to procure badly needed bandages, water, and food.

The "man in white"—Jean-Henri Dunant—was not new to philanthropic endeavors. Born in Geneva, Switzerland, in 1828, he came of a well-to-do family with a strong religious background and a tradition of public service. As a young man Dunant had been an instigator of the movement that created the Young Men's Christian Association (YMCA), which he hoped would promote fellowship and understanding between young men of many cultural backgrounds. Until the age of 30, Dunant was a banker, with business interests throughout Europe and Northern Africa. In June of 1859, these financial affairs took him to Castiglione.

In a sense, Dunant never completely left Solferino. The many startling scenes he witnessed there continued to crowd his mind. "What haunted me," wrote Dunant, "was the memory of the terrible condition of the thousands of wounded." This horrible remembrance of men dying, often for want of the simplest care, inspired him to publish in 1862 a vivid account of the battle and its consequences. The book was called Un Souvenir de Solferino (A Memory of Solferino).

The realistic descriptions, and the compassion for the individual soldier shown in Dunant's book created an immediate sensation in Europe. Un Souvenir de Solferino wasted little space on the traditional "glories" of war; Dunant was more interested in the plight of the "simple troopers . . . [who] suffered without complaint . . . [and] . . . died humbly and quietly." The book advocated a radically new concept of charitable action: that all of the wounded, friend and foe alike, should be cared for. He had been inspired, said Dunant, by the Italian peasant women who murmured "tutti fratelli" (all are brothers) while treating the hated Austrians. Near the end of the book was a brief paragraph, destined to have dramatic impact on the humanitarian efforts of the world: "Would it not be possible," wrote Dunant, "in time of peace and quiet, to form relief societies for the purpose of having care given to the wounded in wartime of zealous, devoted and thoroughly qualified volunteers?"

The simple question may have been overlooked by readers caught up in the battle scenes of Un Souvenir de Solferino. But it caught the imagination of one influential man: Gustav Moynier, a citizen of Geneva who headed the charitable "Committee for the Public Benefit." Moynier introduced a practical direction to Dunant's dreams. He contacted Dunant, and together they established a committee, headed by Moynier, and including the commanding general of the Swiss Army, Guillaume Dufour. Two distinguished doctors, Louis Appia and Theodore Maunoir, completed the "Committee of Five." This committee immediately began plans for an international convention to discuss the treatment of the wounded in wartime.

In February 1863, 16 nations met in Geneva to discuss "the relief of wounded armies in the field." Dunant's proposals were debated and an informal list of agreements was drawn up. This agreement established the national volunteer agencies for relief in war. Then, in August 1864 a second conference was held which produced the international pact, known as the Treaty of Geneva. The treaty rendered "neutral and immune from injury in war the sick and wounded and all who cared for them." To distinguish the neutral medical personnel, supplies and sick, an international badge was needed. Out of respect for Dunant and the country which had been host of the conventions, the design adopted was that of the reversed Swiss flag. Those working under the Treaty of Geneva would thereafter be recognized by the emblem of a red cross on a white flag. The United States signed this treaty on March 16, 1882.

Jean-Henri Dunant's generous dream had been fulfilled, but he obtained no glory or recognition for many years. Dunant had neglected his business interests while promoting the Geneva conventions. By 1867 he was bankrupt and spent most of his remaining life a pauper.

However, Dunant did live to receive, jointly with Frederic Passy, the first Nobel Peace Prize in 1901. It was a fitting tribute to the man who, in the words of Gustav Moynier, "opened the eyes of the blind, moved the hearts of the indifferent, and virtually effected in the intellectual and moral realm the reformation to which [he] aspired."

*In 1864, 11 European nations
agreed to the terms of the Treaty
of Geneva, which established
the Red Cross. This painting,
by Charles Edouard Armand-
Demaresq, shows the ceremony
of signing the treaty.*

rounding countryside for a relief headquarters, finally settling in Belfort. This small border town had heroically withstood Prussian fire for more than eight months. The people were "very poor and their ignorance . . . something deplorable," noted Antoinette Margot. Many of the citizens had never seen paper money— so Barton used only coins—and less than one in 15 could write his name. Her activities were still loosely tied to the Red Cross, but in most cases she used her own judgment to come to terms with the destitution she found. Money was given according to need, solace indiscriminately. Desperate mobs often stormed the home of "Monsieur l'Administrateur" in which she was staying; assistant Margot was "amused . . . to see Miss Barton *protecting her policemen*" and pacifying the crowds with her dignified bearing and calm admonition to "wait a little and be quiet." Barton tried to help the anxious families of prisoners who had lost their means of support and provided some relief for the French leaving German-occupied Alsace. Margot later remarked that she wished "that her own people could see their country-woman at work among European poor as not one European has done."

When the hostilities between France and Prussia ended, and with it the need for Barton's help, her health again declined. Despite the decorations of several governments, she was despondent. Her eyes gave out, her nerves collapsed. She had over-taxed herself in nerve-shattering situations, and she suffered, in part, because she had never really learned to care for herself. Troubled throughout her life by insomnia, she often worked on four or five hours

German soldiers rout French troops at Bazeilles, France, during the Franco-Prussian War.

sleep. A sometimes vegetarian, she took no pains to correctly nourish herself; dinner was too often a large red apple or nothing at all. It is understandable, in the light of this negligence and spiritual decline, that she suffered a relapse into her old nervous disorders.

For a time Barton stayed in Germany. She then traveled with friends throughout Italy, a tour highlighted by a visit to Mt. Vesuvius. In May 1872, she visited the Riviera and traveled via Paris to London. Though somewhat improved, she was still weak, and her restlessness increased daily. She stayed in London for more than a year, made many friends, enjoyed horse shows and Madame Tussaud's, and took part in a congress on prison reform. But all the time she pondered her fate, bemoaned the sacrifice of her time, and let small incidents unduly rankle. For a while she considered writing for newspapers, but she felt too listless. Visits from a niece, from the grand duchess of Baden, who had become her devoted friend, and from Antoinette Margot could not rouse her. Finally, on September 30, 1873, she sailed on the *Parthia* for the United States, still worried and uncertain about her future. "Have ye place, each beloved one, a place in your prayer," she plaintively asked in a poem written aboard the *Parthia*, "Have ye work, my brave countrymen, work for me there?"

Barton hoped to recover her spirits in America. Unfortunately, only a few months after her return, she received word that her sister, Sally, was critically ill. She hurried from Washington, D.C., to Oxford, Massachusetts, only to find that Sally's death had preceded her arrival by hours. This blow was devastating; she collapsed utterly. A year later, still shaky and depressed, she faced the death of Henry Wilson, her political ally and close friend.

Barton was in serious need of a restful atmosphere. Through a young woman in Worcester she learned of a sanitarium at Dansville, New York, where the patients were treated with a popular "water cure." There she found "congenial society, wholesome and simple food, and an atmosphere that believed health to be possible." Her health did indeed improve at Dansville. She eventually bought a house there, and made the small town her home for the next ten years. She participated in plays, attended and gave lectures, went on outings with other patients, and enjoyed her position as the town's most celebrated citizen. And, after one of her lectures, she met one of the most influential people in her life: Julian Hubbell, a young chemistry teacher at Dansville Seminary. They became friends, and when she told him of the Treaty of Geneva and how she hoped for its adoption in the United States, Hubbell asked what he could do to help. "Get a degree in medicine," she advised, and Hubbell complied. He left his teaching position and entered the University of Michigan medical school in 1878.

Julian Hubbell remained uncompromisingly loyal to Barton. When the American Red Cross was established, he became its chief field agent. As such he participated in more actual relief work than she did. His skillful organization and quiet control were directly responsible for much of the success of the early Red Cross. Upon her resignation, he too gave up his career.

In the late 1870s, Barton began to be active again in political affairs. Her long interest in women's rights was re-kindled, especially by Harriet Austin, a doctor at the sanitarium. For a time, Barton adopted the mode of Austin's dress reform— loose, corsetless garments, which included baggy trousers. It pleased her to "shed flannels" and dress "just as free and easy as a gentleman, with lots of pockets, and perambulate around to suit herself." In 1876 she advocated a series of dress reform meetings and helped Susan B. Anthony compile biographies of noted women. In 1878, she participated in suffrage conventions in Washington, D.C., and Rochester, New York.

As Barton's health improved she also renewed her interest in establishing the Red Cross in the United States. She knew that her first step was to obtain the official sanction of the International Red Cross Committee and spent much of 1877 and 1878 corresponding with Dr. Louis Appia about a plan for promoting the Red Cross. Always jealous of her position as sole representative of the cause, Barton was not above discrediting both Charles Bowles and Henry Bellows, early advocates of the Red Cross in America. Bowles is "utterly unreliable . . . and . . . never worthy of confidence," Barton wrote to Appia, and Bellows "wears [his title of representative] as an easy honor, and it never occurs to him that he is retarding the progress of the world." Neither allegation was true. But Barton gained the official blessing of the international committee, and as their representative began her crusade for ratification of the Treaty of Geneva.

Her first concern was to educate the public, for she had found that

Frances Dana Gage (1808-84) found time while raising eight children to write and speak on temperance, slavery, and women's rights. Her antislavery activities in Missouri met with a hostile reception. During the Civil War she helped former slaves adjust to freedom. In her later years she wrote children's stories.

"the knowledge of [the] society and its great objects in this country . . . is almost unknown, and the Red Cross in America is a mystery." In 1878, she published a small pamphlet entitled "What the Red Cross Is." She realized that the American public did not expect to be engaged in another war and emphasized peacetime uses of the Red Cross. Red Cross action against natural disasters had actually been proposed by Henri Dunant in the third edition of *Un Souvenir de Solferino*, but in her pamphlet she gave it priority. "To afford ready succor and assistance in time of national or widespread calamities, to gather and dispense the profuse liberality of our people, without waste of time or material, requires the wisdom that comes of experience and permanent organization."

Barton also began mentioning the Treaty of Geneva in occasional lectures to veterans and local citizens. She wrote persuasively to influential friends, such as Benjamin F. Butler, and former minister to France Elihu B. Washburne. "I am not only a patriotic but a proud woman," she told Washburne, "and our position on this matter is a subject of mortification to me. I am humbled to see the United States stand with the barbarous nations of the world, outside the pale of civilization." Other friends, among them Frances Dana Gage and Mrs. Hannah Shepard, wrote articles advocating establishment of the Red Cross. Barton labored many hours to translate, write, and explain materials on the Red Cross to influential men in New York and Washington.

The same year, 1878, she presented information concerning the Red Cross to President Rutherford B. Hayes. She also delivered an invitation to the United States from International Red Cross president Gustav Moynier to join the association. But she found little enthusiasm in the Hayes administration. A fear of "entangling alliances" with other countries still prevailed and the State Department shied away from permanent treaties. Furthermore, the treaty had previously been submitted by Dr. Bellows, and the Grant Administration had rejected it. Hayes considered the subject closed.

When a Congressional joint resolution to ratify the Treaty of Geneva was tabled early in 1879, she shelved her own plans for a while, traveled between New York State and Washington, D.C., lectured some, and entertained relatives at her Dansville home. But she remained alert for an opportunity, and when James A. Garfield ran for President in 1880, she campaigned in his behalf. With his election that November, she hoped for a more sympathetic administration. To her relief, she found both Garfield and Secretary of State James Blaine interested. Plans were made to submit the treaty to the Senate for ratification, and she continued to lobby senators.

In June 1881, with success in sight, Barton and a few friends formed the first American Association of the Red Cross. She was elected president, an office she originally planned to keep only until the Treaty of Geneva was signed. The organization's main purpose at this stage was to promote adoption of the treaty, without which the body had no international authority or recognition. The first local chapter of the American Red Cross, and the first to give actual aid, was established at Dansville, New York, in August 1881.

Even with the organization established, Barton's trials were not over. The assassination of President Garfield in the summer of 1881 deterred the process of ratification by several months. She also was concerned about the many rival organizations that were mushrooming around her. The "Red Star," "Red Crescent," and "White Cross" all appeared. One group, the "Blue Anchor," posed a threat to the treaty ratification, for several senators' wives belonged to it and were openly hostile to her. The rival charities irritated her, and she let herself indulge in self-pity and undue alarm. "There is in all the world, not one person who will come and work beside me to establish the justice of a good cause," she wrote. "It is only natural that I should long to be out of the human surroundings which care so little for me."

Barton need not have worried so much. The new President, Chester A. Arthur, was an advocate of the Red Cross, and when she called upon the Secretary of State early in 1882 he showed her the treaty, already printed, awaiting only the recommendations of the Senate and official signatures. As she read it, Barton began to weep, for, as a cousin remarked, "her life and hope were bound up in it." On March 16, 1882, she received a note from Senator Elbridge Lapham informing her of "the ratification by the Senate of the Geneva Convention; of the full assent of the United States to the same." "*Laus Deo*," concluded the note, but to Barton it was almost anticlimactic. "I had waited so long," she wrote in her journal, "and was so weak and broken, I could not even feel glad."

Clara Barton's success in securing ratification of the Treaty of Geneva is perhaps her most outstanding achievement. Primarily through her writing, speeches, and dedication the public and U.S. officials came to know of the Red Cross. For six years she persisted in lobbying Congress; the treaty ultimately passed without a dissenting vote. And, although she "could not believe that someone would not rise up" to help her, no one ever did. The American National Red Cross remains a monument to Barton's singular perseverance and her powers of persuasion.

Barton and the Red Cross in Action

Clara Barton was 60 years old when the Treaty of Geneva was ratified by the Senate. She at first considered her work completed. But the immediate demands made on the young American Red Cross changed her mind; she felt it would be foolish to put the Red Cross into other hands.

Barton stamped the early Red Cross decisively with her personality. She was a woman of strong will and deliberate action, with, as biographer Percy Epler states, "a just and accurate estimate of her own power to master a situation." By the 1880s, she was accustomed to being in command. She could, and did, inspire great loyalty—Antoinette Margot's letters to her customarily begin "My own so precious, so precious Miss Barton," or "So dear, so preciously loved Miss Barton"—though some complained that she demanded, rather than deserved the fealty. Barton left no doubt that she alone governed the Red Cross and that all others were subordinate. One of her most loyal aides referred to her as "the Queen."

When many people are closing out their careers, Clara Barton was just beginning her most important work.

She had a sharp intellect, was able to see issues clearly, and was articulate. Although she had clear-cut opinions on nearly every subject, she was loath to force her ideas on others. Dr. Hubbell, writing after her death, maintained that she disliked controversy and would almost never argue, "but when she did speak she could tell more facts to the point . . . with no possibility of misunderstanding than any person I have ever known."

She was confident when she was in control of a situation, but she had difficulty working with others. She was a perfectionist. Determined always to do things in her own way, she early decided "that I must attend to all business myself . . . and learn to do *all* myself." Secretaries and servants came and went, but few ever satisfied her exacting demands. In her own endeavors she could tolerate no rival, but she did not aspire to widespread power.

Privately Barton was often very different from her public image. Criticism was taken with apparent calm and stoicism, but inwardly she burned and fought the temptation "to go from all the world. I think it will come to that someday," she sadly noted, "it is a struggle for me to keep in society at all. I want to leave all." Her temper was also controlled and betrayed itself only by a deepening of her voice and a sharpness in her eyes. She was socially insecure and given to self-dramatization. She often exaggerated her hardships to elicit pity or respect. For example, she frequently spoke of sitting up all night on trains as both a measure of economy and a guard against unnecessary personal luxury, yet her diaries contain numerous references to comfortable berths. Several times she wrote flattering articles about herself, in the third person, which she submitted to various periodicals. In one, written during the Franco-Prussian War, she showed the way she hoped the public would view her: "Miss Clara Barton, scarcely recovered from the fatigues and indispositions resulting from her arduous and useful duties during the War of the Rebellion, was found again foremost bestowing her care upon the wounded with the same assiduity which characterized her among the suffering armies of her own country."

Her depression and insecurity were, in most cases, undetectable to others. What they noticed were her humanitarian feelings and deep and abiding empathy for those who suffered. Her friend, the Grand Duchess Louise, thought of her as "one of those very few persons whose whole being is goodness itself." Biographer and cousin William E. Barton recalled that she "did not merely sympathize with suffering; she suffered." Others were struck by her witty and spontaneous sense of humor. She told one friend that she was more thankful for her sense of humor than for any other quality she possessed, for it had helped her over hard times.

Another of Barton's assets was a keen spirit of objectivity. William Barton noted that she rarely stood on precedent and that she tried to keep an open mind about people, methods of business, and herself. This openness is perceptible in her acceptance of startling changes. Railway travel, typewriters, automobiles, and airplanes were all taken in stride, and when telephones and electric lights became available she had them installed in her home immediately. She welcomed dress reform, prison reform, and other social change. Clara Barton was a determined, sensitive, competent, difficult, and unpredictable woman, and she brought all of these qualities to, and etched them on, the American Red Cross in 1882.

During the years that she was president of the American Red Cross, it was a small but well-known group. Her name lent power and respectability to the Red Cross cause. The list of relief efforts undertaken in those early years is impressive—assistance at the sites of numerous natural disasters, foreign aid to both Russia and Turkey, battlefield relief in the Spanish-American War. She participated in nearly all of the field work, which was her métier, for it combined her humanitarian sentiments with her need to lose herself in her work and the remuneration of praise.

The first work undertaken by the Red Cross in America was actually done prior to the ratification of the Treaty of Geneva. In the fall of 1881, disastrous forest fires swept across Michigan. Local Red Cross chapters at Dansville and Rochester, New York, sent money and materials amounting to $80,000, and Barton directed Julian Hubbell to oversee the work. Thus did Hubbell, still a medical student at the University of Michigan, begin his career as chief field agent for the American Red Cross.

From 1881 on, nearly every year saw the Red Cross actively engaged in the relief of some calamity. In 1882, and again in 1884, the Mississippi and Ohio Rivers flooded, sweeping away valuable property,

In early September 1881, Michigan farmers in "the Thumb" of the State were burning stubble left after the harvest. Aggravated by drought conditions, the fires spread to the dry forests. One estimate at the time stated that an area 100 by 30 kilometers (60 by 20 miles) was burned.

48

HUTS BUILT BY SURVIVORS.

IN THE TRACK OF THE FLAMES

MAIMED BOYS

A STRICKEN FAMILY

leaving hundreds destitute and homeless. Relief centers were established
in Cincinnati and Evansville, Indiana, and the Red Cross steamers, the
Josh V. Throop and *Mattie Belle*, co-
operated with government relief
boats to supply sufferers cut off by
water. All along the rivers, families
were furnished with fuel, clothing
and food, or cash. The Red Cross
also undertook to relieve starving
and sick animals by contributing
oats, hay, corn, and medicine. Lumber, tools, and seeds were left to
help the stricken rebuild their lives.
Barton herself supervised the work
on the *Mattie Belle* as it plowed its
way between the cities of St. Louis
and New Orleans.

The American Red Cross did not
attempt to supply every need in
every instance, nor did it try to aid
the victims of every calamity. A
notable case in which the Red Cross
declined to give aid occurred in 1887.
A severe drought had plagued the
people of northwestern Texas for
several years; State and Federal aid
had been denied and in desperation a
representative of the stricken area
applied to Barton for relief. She
went directly to the scene, but she
determined that what was needed
was not Red Cross aid but an organized drive for public contributions.
Through the *Dallas News* she adver-
tised for help and was delighted to
find a quick response.

Besides flood and fire relief, the
young American Red Cross helped
tornado victims in Louisiana and
Alabama in 1883 and contributed in
the relief of an earthquake at
Charleston, South Carolina, in 1886.
When a tornado struck Mount Vernon, Illinois, in February 1888, Barton and her co-workers organized the

49

inhabitants so effectively that they needed to stay at the scene only two weeks.

An outbreak of yellow fever in Jacksonville, Florida, also in 1888, precipitated the first use of trained Red Cross nurses, many of whom worked heroically. In one instance, ten of them jumped from a moving train to enter the small town of Macclenny, Florida, whose rail service had been stopped because of the fever's epidemic proportions. But unfortunately the Jacksonville episode was not an entirely happy one. Barton had a lifelong inability to pick qualified subordinates; in this case the man she chose to supervise the nurses—a Colonel Southmayd of the New Orleans Red Cross—had extremely poor judgment. Southmayd found the Jacksonville workers to be "earnest and warm-hearted," but all evidence is to the contrary. Some nurses refused to work for three dollars a day when they could get four dollars in private hospitals. One got drunk on the whiskey used as medicine, another was arrested for theft, and several were accused of immoral conduct. Southmayd staunchly refused to remove the offending nurses, and for a time the incident put an unfortunate stigma on Red Cross workers. It also served to strengthen Clara Barton's determination to oversee personally as much Red Cross field work as possible.

The most celebrated peacetime relief work undertaken by the young American Red Cross was at Johnstown, Pennsylvania, in 1889. Johnstown, at the point where Stony Creek joins the Conemaugh River, often endured spring floods, but in May 1889 the rains were unusually heavy. After several days low-lying parts of Johnstown lay under 1 to 4 meters (3 to 13 feet) of water. Then a dam broke in the mountains 16 kilometers (10 miles) from the city. A wall of water, 9 meters (30 feet) high, rushed down to kill 2,200 people and destroy millions of dollars in property.

Barton arrived in Johnstown five days after the tragedy on the first train that got through. She immediately began work, using a tent as living and office space, and a dry goods box as a desk. From that desk she administered a program that amounted to half a million dollars, conducted a publicity campaign, and joined forces with the other charitable societies working in Johnstown. One of her aides recalled the long hours and complex work that characterized their five months in Johnstown and noted that through it all she remained "calm, benign, tireless and devoted."

Barton's first concern was a warehouse for Red Cross supplies and under her direction workmen erected one in four days. She then turned to alleviating the acute housing shortage. Hotels, two stories high and containing more than 30 rooms each, were built and fully furnished to serve as temporary shelters. Crews of men were organized to clean up the wreckage, while women volunteered to oversee the distribution of clothing and other necessities. As in all its work, the Red Cross tried to supply jobs and a spirit of self-help along with material assistance.

Clara Barton's organization was only one of many that came to the aid of Johnstown, but its contribution was outstanding for its quick thinking and tireless energy. Gov. James A. Beaver of Pennsylvania noted in a

Floodwaters roamed through Johnstown, Pennsylvania, in 1889, destroying a great number of homes and businesses. More than 2,200 persons lost their lives.

51

letter of appreciation to the Red Cross that "she was among the first to arrive on the scene of calamity. . . . She was also the last of the ministering spirits to leave the scene of her labors." The city of Johnstown scarcely knew how to express its thanks. "We cannot thank Miss Barton in words," an editorial in the *Johnstown Daily Tribune* stated. "Hunt the dictionaries of all languages through and you will not find the signs to express our appreciation of her and her work. Try to describe the sunshine. Try to describe the starlight. Words fail."

Field work took up a large portion of Barton's time in the 1880s, but she was able to pursue some other interests and obligations. During 1883, for example, she was superintendent of the Women's Reformatory Prison at Sherborn, Massachusetts. She undertook the position at the request of former general, now Gov. Benjamin F. Butler, but she took it reluctantly. Her administration was characterized by the extension of dignity and education to inmates, rather than punishment. She found the work annoying and depressing, and she was glad to leave it and get back to the Red Cross.

Between the burdensome paper work and correspondence of the Red Cross and actual relief work, Barton found time to be the official American representative to four International Red Cross conferences between 1882 and 1902. She enjoyed these trips to Europe, for they gave her a chance to see friends and to be honored, as she always was by court and convention. The international congress of 1884, at Geneva, was especially memorable. An "American Amendment" to the Geneva Treaty was adopted, and, as the head of the newest signatory power in the Red Cross she was the center of attention. The amendment sanctioned Red Cross work in peacetime calamities and was the direct result of her activities in the United States. The congress cheered as she was praised as having "the skill of a statesman, the heart of a woman, and the 'final perserverance [*sic*] of the saints.' "

Barton was also concerned with planning a national headquarters for the American Red Cross. In the 1880s and early 1890s Red Cross headquarters were located at various spots in Washington, D.C. After 1891, however, plans were made to build a permanent home for the organization. Situated at Glen Echo, Maryland, a short distance outside Washington, the new building served both as office and home for Barton and her staff.

What few hours she could spare from Red Cross activities she devoted to raising the status of women. She was proud that the Red Cross embodied many of her beliefs. In the last two decades of the 19th century, she continued to speak at rallies and join conventions promoting women's rights. Her lecture topics generally centered on philanthropic work done by women, but she spoke out most vehemently on female suffrage. She was incensed that the decision to let women vote hinged upon the assent of male legislators, but she remained optimistic about the ultimate outcome. She told one lecture audience that "there is no one to give woman the right to govern herself. But in one way or another, sooner or later, she is coming to it. And the number of thoughtful and right-minded men who will oppose will be much smaller than we think, and when it is really an accomplished fact, all women will wonder, as I have done, what the objection ever was."

Barton's prestige lent respect to the feminist cause, and she was in much demand as a lecturer and author. In 1888 alone, she spoke in Montclair, New Jersey; Dansville, New York; Boston and Dorchester, Massachusetts, and was a vice president and featured speaker at the First International Woman's Suffrage Conference in Washington, D.C.

Red Cross activities in the 1890s followed much the same pattern as those of the previous decade. Hubbell and Barton oversaw relief to tornado victims in Pomeroy, Iowa, in 1893, and helped those ravaged by a hurricane off the coast of South Carolina in late 1893 and 1894. When news of a famine in Russia reached the United States, the American Red Cross obtained supplies, including 500 carloads of corn given by Iowa farmers, and shipped them to Russia. The actual relief was relatively little, but it pioneered the concept of peacetime foreign aid.

American money and supplies also were used to help victims of religious wars in Turkey and Armenia during 1896. Although Turkey had signed the Treaty of Geneva, Red Cross efforts were at first resisted there. Under strong pressure from the American public, however, Barton and field workers of the American Red Cross sailed for Turkey. They gained admittance to the country and spent ten months helping the wounded and distributing tools and medical supplies. It was, in many ways, a harrowing experience, and the safety of the Americans was repeatedly threatened. At least one of

Despite bouts of nervousness Clara Barton enjoyed public speaking and was in great demand as a lecturer, talking either about her Civil War experiences or women's rights.

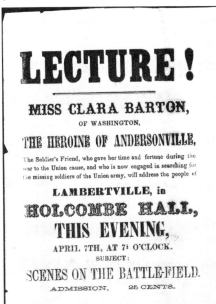

LECTURE !

MISS CLARA BARTON,

OF WASHINGTON,

THE HEROINE OF ANDERSONVILLE,

The Soldier's Friend, who gave her time and fortune during the war to the Union cause, and who is now engaged in searching for the missing soldiers of the Union army, will address the people of

LAMBERTVILLE, in

HOLCOMBE HALL,

THIS EVENING,

APRIL 7TH, AT 7½ O'CLOCK.

SUBJECT:

SCENES ON THE BATTLE-FIELD.

ADMISSION,   25 CENTS.

Barton's biographers, Blanche Colton Williams, thought that the Armenian relief work was the height of Barton's achievement.

Despite all of Clara Barton's peacetime achievements, the Red Cross remained officially connected with the military, its chief function being to give medical aid in time of war. The Spanish-American War in 1898 provided the first chance for the American Red Cross to serve in this official capacity. Unfortunately, the Red Cross effort was fragmented, marked by contention and controversy, and it ultimately led to the entire reorganization of the Red Cross in America.

The Red Cross, under Barton, sent various types of assistance to Cuba. The earliest efforts, starting in January 1898, were in behalf of the thousands of Cuban nationalists who had been herded into concentration camps by the Spanish colonial government. Barton was giving civilian aid in Cuba when the battleship USS *Maine* blew up. When war was declared on April 25, 1898, Barton and her small crew went to work in field hospitals and hospital boats. She was distressed to find that once again the Army Medical Department had sent inadequate personnel, and that cots, food, and bandages were all lacking. "It is the Civil War all over," she lamented, "no improvement in a third of a century."

Meanwhile a controversy of distressing proportions had developed within the Red Cross. A powerful local auxiliary of the American Red Cross, in New York, felt that the handful of workers led by 77-year-old Barton was not adequate to meet the needs of troops and civilians. This chapter, which became known as the Red Cross Relief Committee of New York, was, in many ways, more powerful than Barton's small national organization. Where Barton's group had concentrated on "hand to mouth" relief efforts—those in which funds and supplies were given as soon as received—the New York organization had gathered stores and funds, and had established a hospital and school for nurses, and formed nearly 200 relief auxiliaries. It collected and shipped many more articles to Cuba during 1898 than did the national society and sent several times the number of trained nurses and doctors. The Red Cross Relief Committee of New York was professionally run and its leaders were distressed by Barton's lowscale personal style, which had changed little since the Civil War.

As she tried to retain control of the relief efforts, the New York group fought for government sanction as the sole agency of the Red Cross working in Cuba. Surgeon General George Sternberg favored the New Yorkers, but the secretary of state upheld Barton's claim. Little was resolved and the two organizations continued to work independently. When the New York Committee requested an accounting of funds spent in Cuba, of which it had supplied the bulk, Barton wired to a subordinate: "If insisted on refuse co-operation with [New York] committee." Rivalry and jealousy took the place of collaboration.

Barton viewed the New Yorkers as insurgents trying to usurp her glory. "The world in general is after me in many ways," she wrote. "I only wish I could draw out of it *all*." She believed that the New Yorkers' function should have been one of supply

Continues on page 56

Scenes from the Spanish-American War

The Spanish-American War took place between April 25, 1898, and August 13, 1898. Battles were fought in the Philippines and Puerto Rico, but most of the fighting was in Cuba. Public reaction to the oppressive Spanish rule of Cuba initiated the conflict, when the battleship USS *Maine* exploded in February 1898. Although it was never proven, the widespread belief was that the ship had been torpedoed by the Spaniards. Clara Barton visited the *Maine* a few days before the disaster, and was nearby when the explosion occurred: "The heavy clerical work of that fifteenth day of February held [us] . . . busy at our writing tables until late at night. The house had grown still; the noises on the streets were dying away, when suddenly the table shook from under our hands, the great glass door opening on to the . . . sea flew open; everything in the room was in motion or out of place, the deafening roar of such a burst of thunder as perhaps one never heard before, and off to the right, out over the bay, the air was filled with a blaze of light, and this in turn filled with black specks like huge specters flying in all directions. A few hours later came . . . news of the *Maine*.

"We proceeded to the Spanish hospital San Ambrosia, to find thirty to forty wounded— bruised, cut, burned; they had been crushed by timbers, cut by iron, scorched by fire, and blown sometimes high in the air, sometimes driven down through the red-hot furnace room and out into the water, senseless, to be picked up by some boat and gotten ashore. . . . Both men and officers are very reticent in regard to the cause, but all declare it could not have been the result of an internal explosion . . . ."

The earliest efforts of the Red Cross in Cuba were to aid the civilian *reconcentrados* who were being detained by the Spaniards. Medical aid, clothing, and food were distributed, and hospitals and orphanages established. When fighting broke out, however, the Red Cross moved to supply the needs of the wounded. Clara Barton described the scene of one hospital camp in July 1898: "[We] reached here [General William Shafter's headquarters] yesterday. Five more of us came today by army wagon and on foot. Eight hundred wounded have reached this hospital from front since Sunday morning. Surgeons and little squads have worked day and night. Hospital accommodations inadequate and many wounded on water-soaked ground without shelter or blankets. Our supplies a godsend. Have made barrels of gruel and malted milk and given food to many soldiers who have had none in three days."

Barton, as always, pursued her work with impartiality: Cubans, Spaniards, and Americans all received her care. Henry Lathrop, a doctor who worked for the Red Cross Committee of New York felt this had a direct bearing on the outcome of the war. "Miss Barton was everywhere among the Spanish soldiers, sick, wounded and well. She was blessed by the enemies of her country and I seriously doubt if [General] Shafter himself did more to conquer Santiago with his men, muskets and cannon, than this woman. . . . The wounded men told their comrades about the kind treatment they had received at the hands of the Americans, and the news spread through the Army like wild-fire, completely changing the conditions. Those that preferred death to surrender were now anxious to surrender."

Despite such words of praise, Barton encountered some of the same prejudices that had hindered her work during the Civil War. Lucy Graves, Barton's secretary, recorded that "some of the surgeons called on us; all seemed interested in the Red Cross, but none thought that a woman nurse would be in place in a soldier's hospital. Indeed, very much out of place." Most of the doctors changed their tune and were very happy to receive Barton's help and supplies during a battle. Another grateful recipient of Red Cross supplies was Col. Theodore Roosevelt, commander of the celebrated "Rough Riders." One day Roosevelt showed up at Red Cross headquarters requesting food and supplies for his sick men. "Can I buy them from the Red Cross?" he asked.

"Not for a million dollars," Barton said.

The colonel looked disappointed. He was proud of his men, and said they needed these things. "How can I get them?" he insisted. "I must have proper food for my sick men."

"Just ask for them, colonel," she said.

"Then I do ask for them" he said.

"Before we had recovered from our surprise," related Barton, "the incident was closed by the future President of the United States slinging the big sack over his shoulders, striding off . . . through the jungle."

Probably no thrill in Barton's life was greater than the honor accorded her after the fall of Santiago, Cuba. When this city was conquered, the first vessel to enter the harbor was the Red Cross relief ship *The State of Texas*. A proud Barton stood on the deck of the ship and led the little band of Red Cross workers in singing the Doxology and "America."

and support for her own group, and she could not understand why they criticized her for rushing off to give relief rather than staying at home to direct the organization. And she did not appreciate the problems that her absence from Washington caused. The Army, irritated by the internal strife in the Red Cross, supported neither group and offered little cooperation. Thus, the relief effort in Cuba ended with minimal relief given and a divided American Red Cross.

Storm and Controversy

To many members of the American Red Cross the work in the Spanish-American War exemplified all that was wrong with their organization: lack of coordination, and the arbitrary and short-sighted rule of Clara Barton. Yet she seemed perfectly satisfied. In her book, *The Red Cross in Peace and War* (1898), she contended that the Red Cross took a major and laudatory part in the hospital operations in Cuba. She made no attempts at conciliation or compromise with her critics and continued to run the American Red Cross in the same individualistic style.

It came as no surprise to those who knew Barton when she rushed once more to a scene of a disaster. In September 1900 a hurricane and tidal wave nearly submerged Galveston, Texas, and Barton, though 80 years old, did not hesitate. Six weeks later she returned to Glen Echo laden with praise and testimonials that her achievements in Galveston were "greater than the conquests of nations or the inventions of genius."

Her desire to remain in the field stymied the growth of the American Red Cross because she failed to delegate authority. When she spent six

Clara Barton insisted that assistance and relief during peacetime become a standard Red Cross practice. Here the Red Cross gives help after the hurricane at Galveston, Texas, in 1900.

weeks or ten months away from Washington she left behind no organization to continue day-to-day activities, solicit contributions, or expand programs. Local chapters felt alienated from the national group and resented that they often provided the material support but saw little of the praise. One critic, Sophia Welk Royce Williams, wrote: "The National Red Cross Association in this country has been Miss Clara Barton, and Miss Clara Barton has been the National Red Cross Society. . . . [The Red Cross] has been of great service to suffering humanity, but when one asks for detailed reports, for itemized statements of disbursements . . . these things either do not exist or are not furnished." The better course, Williams believed, would have been for the Red Cross to adopt the organization of the Sanitary Commission. Barton's group clearly lacked a national organization, a national board, and reports that would stand as models and guides for relief work.

If the organization suffered, the quality of relief did not. At least one initially skeptical correspondent saw much to praise in the one-woman show. While visiting the hurricane-devastated Sea Islands in South Carolina, Joel Chandler Harris wrote that the Red Cross's "strongest and most admirable feature is extreme simplicity. The perfection of its machinery is shown by the apparent absence of all machinery. There are no exhibitions of self-importance. There is no display—no tortuous cross-examination of applicants—no needless delay. And yet nothing is done blindly, or hastily or indifferently."

What Harris also saw was a concerted effort to assist without the demeaning effects of charity. Barton developed a knack for leaving a disaster area at the right time: "It is indispensable that one know when to end such relief, in order to avoid first the weakening of effort and powers for self-sustenance; second the encouragement of a tendency to beggary and pauperism."

During her 23-year tenure as president of the American Red Cross, Clara Barton was both its chief asset and its greatest liability. As founder and president she promoted the Red Cross cause with all of her considerable talent, and she brought zeal and idealism to Red Cross relief work. At the same time, her domineering, and sometimes high-handed, ways hindered organizational growth. As Red Cross historian Foster Rhea Dulles notes, her methods of administration were not always based on sound business practices and did not command the confidence of many people who might have given the association broader support.

Barton's failure to delegate authority and to acknowledge popular contributions more formally provided the basis for the criticism that overwhelmed her between 1900 and 1904. It also accounted, at least in part, for the bitter personal attacks that led to a deepening feud between her friends and foes. Despite her adaptability in earlier days, it was almost impossible for her to adjust to the new conditions of Red Cross activity.

The group that opposed her was made up of prominent Red Cross workers and was led by Mabel Boardman, an able and ambitious society woman. Boardman's group was anxious to see the Red Cross reorganized and their cause gained momentum during 1900 and 1901. Barton refused to consider it. Instead she divided the Red Cross into camps of "friends" and "enemies." She accused her foes of seeking power and of trying to gain admission to the royal courts of Europe through the Red Cross. At the annual meeting in 1902 after anticipating a move to force her resignation, she rallied her forces and emerged with greater powers and the presidency for life. "Perhaps not quite wise," she wrote, "in view of ugly remarks that may be made." For the opposition, who believed that the new charter had been railroaded through, this was the last straw.

After the 1902 meeting Barton thought that "the clouds of despair and dread" had finally lifted, but events moved swiftly against her. Boardman's group succeeded in convincing President Theodore Roosevelt that she was mishandling what was, by then, a quasi-governmental office. On January 2, 1903, his secretary wrote to Barton stating that the President and Cabinet would not serve—as all of his predecessors had—on a committee of consultation for the Red Cross. The President directed his secretary to announce publicly his withdrawal from the Red Cross board.

Barton was humiliated by the President's clear endorsement of the opposition faction, but she was absolutely devastated by the subsequent decision to have a government committee investigate the Red Cross. The official charges maintained that proper books of accounts were not kept, that funds and contributions were not always reported to the Red Cross treasurer, and that money was distributed in an arbitrary and inconsistent manner. There was also a question about a tract of land located in Indiana that had been donated to the Red Cross but never reported to the organizational board. The charges were serious. Barton knew that she had often used only her own judgment to apportion relief funds and that she seldom kept accurate records in the field. She was so much a part of her organization that she often failed to differentiate between personal and Red Cross expenses— using her own funds for relief work and donations for private needs. Unofficially her foes also contended that she was too old and infirm to lead the Red Cross; they felt new blood was desperately needed.

Barton was deeply wounded by the controversy swirling around her. A loyal and patriotic woman, she felt that her friends and country had deserted her and that she had been scrupulously honest. For a time, she even considered fleeing to Mexico, but she was dissuaded by friends. Though the investigating committee dropped the charges, thereby completely exonerating her from any wrongdoing, she felt the indignity for the rest of her life.

It is ironic that the qualities Clara Barton cherished and exemplified most—loyalty and friendship, honesty and individual action—were the very ones in question during the investigation. She could not admit defeat, or even unconscious wrongdoing of any kind. There is no question that the time had come for her to give up leadership of the Red Cross, but it is sad that her foes could not have eased her out more gracefully or handled the situation with tact and sympathy. In May 1904, at the age of 83, Clara Barton resigned as president of the American Red Cross.

Theodore Roosevelt

In retirement she broke all ties with the Red Cross but retained a lively interest in its activities. She often felt bitter about the events that preceded her resignation, and she particularly resented the way in which new Red Cross members were prejudiced against her—"ignorant of every fact, simply enemies by transmission." She was also critical of the way in which the new Red Cross leaders approached relief work, especially during the San Francisco earthquake of 1906. A small note of satisfaction is detected in a diary entry: "The President has withdrawn the distribution of public moneys contributed for San Francisco from the Red Cross. . . . He finds he made a mistake in giving too much power to the Red Cross."

Still, she usually wished the best for the Red Cross. Her "one great desire" was to "leave my little immigrant of twenty-seven years ago a great National Institution." And she hoped her successors would be "freed from the severity of toil, the anguish of perplexity, uncertainty, misunderstanding, and often privations, which have been ours in the past."

One of her last public efforts was the formation, in 1905, of the National First Aid Society, which helped establish community aid programs. "I thought I had done my country and its people the most humane service it would ever be in my power to offer," commented Barton, "But . . . [the Red Cross] reached only a certain class. All the accidents concerning family life . . . manufactories and railroads . . . were not within its province. Hence the necessity and the opportunity for this broader work covering all."

Continues on page 62

59

Clara Barton was one of the most decorated women in United States history. In appreciation of her courageous humanitarian services she received ten badges and medals from foreign countries. Many of these medals were conferred upon her in person by such leaders as Kaiser Wilhelm I of Germany and his daughter Louise, the grand duchess of Baden. In one instance, Abdul Mamed, the sultan of Turkey, was so impressed with Barton's methods of relief work that he accompanied his medal with a message to the State Department: if America desired to send further relief to Turkey, please send Clara Barton and her workers.

Although she was never officially honored by the United States government, Barton received many private medals and honorary memberships from American organizations; the Loyal Legion of Women of Washington, D.C., the *Waffengenossen* (German-American soldiers who took part in the Franco-Prussian War), the Vanderbilt Benevolent Association of South Carolina, and the Ladies of Johnstown, Pennsylvania, were among those that honored Clara Barton in this way. One award she particularly valued was a medal presented to her in 1882 by the International Committee of the Red Cross, when America adopted the Treaty of Geneva. Barton was also proud of the numerous "royal jewels" which were gifts of her friends the grand duchess of Baden, and Augusta, empress of Germany. Barton's favorite among these was a large amethyst, carved in the shape of a pansy.

She enjoyed her decorations without apology. They were in old boxes inside a "simple little wicker satchel," and she rarely let them out of her sight. She even took them with her when she traveled. Visitors to her Glen Echo home were always eager to see the medals, and Barton was eager to show them. She would spend hours telling stories about the decorations beginning with a gold Masonic emblem. "My father gave it to me when I started for the front (during the Civil War)," Barton would say, "and I have no doubt that it protected me on many an occasion."

Many of her favorite tales involved the Iron Cross of Germany; one of these took place in Massachusetts. She had been invited to a ball

Pansy carved from amethyst

Iron Cross of Imperial Germany

International Red Cross medal

Smoky topaz with pearls

Cross of Imperial Russia

Masonic emblem

at which she wore a number of her medals. "I was being whirled around the ballroom by some gallant or other when I saw three German officers looking curiously at me as I passed. I wondered for a moment but promptly forgot about it until, as we swung around the room again . . . the music suddenly stopped short. Everyone was gazing about bewilderedly, when I saw three officers advancing toward me and stopping, in front of me, gave the full German military salute. I was thoroughly astonished, but rallied enough to return the salute, which I fortunately remembered." Barton thought the whole situation highly amusing. "They did not know who I was," she concluded, "they simply dared not pass the Iron Cross without saluting it."

Another humorous incident involved one of Barton's royal jewels. Many of the decorations were valuable in themselves, for they were fashioned from gold and silver and set with diamonds, sapphires, and exquisite enamel work. However, one brooch in particular was precious: a large smoky topaz set in gold, and surrounded by 24 perfectly matched pearls, the gift of the grand duchess of Baden. Once Barton took the brooch to Tiffany's in New York for repair. She was dressed simply, as was her habit, and an efficient floorwalker suspected that perhaps she was not the rightful owner of the jewel. Eventually a manager was brought in who recognized Barton and cleared up the matter. He then expressed his admiration of the topaz brooch, especially the 24 pearls. Clara Barton liked to remember how astonished the suspicious floorwalker was that "such a shabby woman should own such remarkable jewels."

Barton enjoyed wearing her decorations as much as talking about them and she nearly always pinned on several before addressing an audience, or attending a meeting. In her later years she was often seen weeding the garden or milking the cows with one or two medals attached to her cotton workdress. On one occasion she was nearly weighted down by simultaneously wearing the Iron Cross, the Red Cross of Geneva, the Masonic badge, the Silver Cross of Serbia, and the extremely heavy Empress Augusta Medal. Said Barton: "They do brighten up the old dress."

The business of First Aid took up much of her time, but she continued her other interests. She attended and spoke at suffrage conventions and held a party for 400 feminists at her Glen Echo home. But she viewed with a jaundiced eye the arrival of the "suffragettes." "Huge hats, dangerous hatpins, hobble and harem skirts," she observed in her diary of 1911, "the conduct of the Suffragettes are [sic] hard to defend." She mourned the death of Susan B. Anthony in 1906, and gave her final public remarks on behalf of women as a tribute to Anthony's memory: "A few days ago someone said in my presence that every woman in the world should stand with bared head before Susan B. Anthony. Before I had time to think I said, 'And every man as well.' I would not retract the words. I believe her work is more for the welfare of man than for that of woman herself. Man is trying to carry the burdens of the world alone. When he had the efficient help of woman he should be glad, and he will be. Just now it is new and strange, and men cannot comprehend what it would mean. But when such help comes, and men are used to it, they will be grateful for it. The change is not far away. This country is to know woman suffrage, and it will be a glad and proud day when it comes."

Barton was also kept busy by the work of two households—the Glen Echo house and a summer home in North Oxford, Massachusetts. She worked in the gardens, put up fruit and vegetables, did her own laundry, and even milked the cows. She also continued her voluminous correspondence, and wrote a slim autobiographical volume, *The Story of My*

In the years that Clara Barton spent at Glen Echo, she came to love her house and yard. Here Dr. Hubbell, Mary Hines, the housekeeper, and Clara Barton relax at the dinner table.

Childhood. The book, published in 1907, was intended to be the first of a series. The work of writing was taxing, however, and she never finished the second volume. But she remained active. "I still work many hours, and walk many miles," she proudly told friends in 1909. In her diary she wrote that she had had "a hard day's work—but I am so thankful—so grateful that I can do it, and am not a helpless invalid to be waited on."

Barton knew she was aging but fought it. Privately she conceded that "there is a lack of coordination between the brain and the limbs," but publicly she resented any allusion to her age. She disliked giving away recent photographs of herself and wished people would accept pictures of her in "strong middle life." She also fooled nature—and many people—by artistically covering her age. A young relative was amazed to find that Aunt Clara "was very particular about her make-up and in those days there were few people who dared use creams and rouge and powder, but Aunt Clara used them skillfully and the result was most amazingly good. She looked years younger when she had finished . . . and her eyebrows were treated with a pencil, if you please.

"Next came the combing of her coal black hair which, by the way, had been dyed. Mother told me once when she was with Aunt Clara when she was sick for a long period and couldn't have her hair attended to, it was lovely and white, but she would not have it so and wore it dyed black to the very last.

"After her face and hair were finished . . . [she] put on her waist, but before buttoning it down the front, she stuffed tissue paper all across the front to make a nice rounded bust."

She was, in many ways, an eccentric figure. Visitors were amused to see her weed the garden, her chest plastered with the decorations of foreign governments. She was always an individual in matters of dress, but her costumes became more unusual in her later years. Her favorite dress color was green and she enjoyed wearing a dash of red. One outfit had five ill-matching shades of green for skirt, sleeves, collar and bodice, two kinds of lace, red ribbon, "and about the bottom . . . was a strip of the most awful old motheaten beaver fur, about six inches wide." Financially, she was quite well off, but in the best New England tradition she practiced economy in all things. When a part of her dress wore out, she apparently replaced it with whatever material was on hand.

Most of Clara Barton's friends and family died before her, and in her last years she was often lonely. She sometimes thought her achievements were worthless beside the importance of friendship. "*What matters the praise of the world?*" Barton asked herself in her journal on February 6, 1907, "*and what matter after we leave it especially? How hollow is that thing called fame.*"

Barton's loneliness heightened what had been a mild interest in spiritualism. She used faith healers and urged them on others. From 1903 on she was a champion of Christian Science and was an outspoken defender of Mary Baker Eddy, the founder of Christian Science. She also dabbled in astrology and became a firm believer in spiritualistic seances. Much of her time after 1907 was spent in the company of a medium. With complete sincerity Barton recorded conversations with Lincoln, Grant, and Sherman, with her family, and with old friends Susan B. Anthony, President McKinley, and Empress Augusta of Germany. She relied on these "spirits" for advice and persuaded Dr. Hubbell to depend on them, too. This had unfortunate repercussions. After Barton's death, Hubbell was taken in by a woman who claimed to have made contact with Barton's spirit. Hubbell was so under the influence of this woman that he actually gave her the house at Glen Echo. It was several years and court cases later before he got the house back.

Clara Barton died on April 12, 1912, at the age of 90. She had endured double-pneumonia twice in one year and was too weak to recover fully. Her last words, recalled from a favorite poem, were "Let me go, let me go."

She was a remarkable woman. She was neither the Christ-like figure Dr. Hubbell idolized, nor the grasping Red Cross potentate that others saw. She was an individual capable of firm action, strong beliefs, and an ability to see a need clearly and fulfill it. To everything she did—schoolteaching, Civil War aid, and Red Cross relief—she brought strong idealism and unfailing energy. She was truly exceptional.

In 1902 Clara Barton was asked to be commencement speaker for Philadelphia's Blockley Hospital nursing class. Here she poses with the graduates for the camera. By her eighty-first year she had become a national figure despite the mounting criticism of her management of the American Red Cross.

65

3

Clara Barton's house in Glen Echo owes its existence to two unrelated facts: The 1889 Johnstown Flood and a plan for a housing development at Glen Echo. In 1890, two brothers, Edwin and Edward Baltzley, decided to develop a cultural and intellectual residential community in Glen Echo. The next year they established a branch of the National Chautauqua, an association dedicated to education and productive recreation. The Baltzley brothers approached Clara Barton and offered her a plot of land and the workmen necessary to build a structure if she would locate in their community. They hoped that the attraction of such a well-known personality as Barton would be a testimonial to the soundness of their enterprise.

The proposal suited Barton perfectly, for she was looking for a location on which she could build a new headquarters building for the Red Cross. After the Johnstown Flood she and Dr. Julian Hubbell had had one of the Red Cross warehouses dismantled and the lumber shipped to Washington D.C., where she hoped to use it for the construction of the new headquarters building. The Baltzleys' offer came just at the right moment and she accepted immediately. Although it was understood that it was Red Cross property, the land was deeded directly to her. The whole transaction was typical of the confusion that Barton allowed to exist between her private possessions and those of the Red Cross; she could never clearly separate the two.

Dr. Hubbell supervised the construction of the building, clearly following the lines of the Johnstown structure. Here, however, he added an extra flourish: a third floor "lantern" room over the central well. In the summer of 1891 Barton and Hubbell moved in, but she found daily travel to Washington, D.C., every day too taxing and decided to use the house at Glen Echo strictly as a warehouse.

In 1897 electric trolley lines made Glen Echo more accessible to Washington, and she decided once again to try living in Glen Echo. Extensive remodeling made the house livable. A stone facade originally built so that the Red Cross headquarters would harmonize with the nearby Chautauqua buildings, which were never built, was removed and the house was painted a warm yellow with brown trim.

The Glen Echo house was the headquarters of the American National Red Cross from 1897 to 1904. As such it was the scene of much official activity. But it was also a quiet retreat, a farm, and a home. Chickens and a cow provided food for the household that usually in-

At the left is an exterior view of the house at Glen Echo. The top view on this page is of the center hall with its balconies. The front parlor contains furniture that originally belonged to Clara Barton. The portrait is of her cat Tommy.

Pages 66 and 67: Clara Barton and Red Cross workers have a picnic in Tampa, Florida, in 1898.

cluded eight or nine staff members. Frequent overnight guests and indigents sheltered by Clara Barton swelled this number further. Her horses, Baba and Prince, were housed in a stable, and cats Tommy and Pussy roamed the grounds. A large vegetable garden furnished fresh produce. The grounds were a profusion of flowers and vegetables mixed together. Visitors noted that carrots and beets edged the walkway out to the trolley stop. Beds of marigolds, corn, roses, and tomatoes grew together. Of particular pride to the owner were the two varieties of Clara Barton rose that were developed independently by two nurserymen: Conrad Jones in West Grove, Pennsylvania, and Mr. Hofmeister in Cincinnati, Ohio. Strawberry plants sent to her by the grateful farmers of Galveston, Texas, in appreciation of her services after the disastrous hurricane and tidal wave in 1900 provided great desserts each June.

In 1909 Barton deeded the house to Dr. Hubbell—perhaps in fear that the Red Cross might try to reclaim the building after her death. When she died in 1912, Dr. Hubbell together with Mrs. John Logan and Gen. W. H. Sears formed the Clara Barton Memorial Association. They hoped to turn the house into a monument to Barton's memory. They sold memberships in the association to finance the maintenance of the property but the response was poor, and they soon ran into financial problems.

The solution to their problems appeared to be at hand when Mabelle Rawson Hirons came on the scene. A native of North Oxford, Massachusetts, she was an acquaintance of Clara Barton and thus known to Hubbell and his colleagues. She claimed that Barton had appeared to her at a seance and told her to go to Washington and take charge of the Glen Echo house. This message "from the beyond" and Mrs. Hirons' assurances that she was wealthy and would take care of all the financial problems were all that the Memorial Association members needed to receive her with open arms. Even her demand that Dr. Hubbell sign the deed over to her raised no doubts.

Within a short time it became startlingly apparent that Mrs. Hirons was not about to pay off the debts of the house. Instead she was using the house to pay off *her* debts by selling Barton's own furniture and renting out rooms. Dr. Hubbell was evicted by Mrs. Hirons and abandoned by members of the Memorial Association who were disgusted with his failure to understand what Mrs. Hirons was doing. He had to fend for himself until a Mr. and Mrs.

Canada, owners of a local grocery store, took him in. They persuaded him to sue Mrs. Hirons in 1922, and four years later the courts returned the house to him.

Dr. Hubbell died in 1929 and left the house to two of his nieces, Rena and Lena Hubbell. Only Rena lived in the house, which she ran as a rooming house. In 1942 she and her sister sold it to Josephine Frank Noyes, who had come to Washington from Iowa. Mrs. Noyes and her sister Henrietta Frank continued to run it as a rooming house. They also urged people to come and see "Clara Barton's House." They took care of the remaining original furniture and even managed to acquire some of the pieces that Mrs. Hirons had sold.

In 1958 Mrs. Noyes died and left the property to her four sisters: Frances Frank, Henrietta Frank, Katherine Frank Bronson, and Sarah Frank Rhodes. By 1963 the sisters, being quite elderly, felt that the house was too big for them to keep up and decided to sell it. The amusement park next door offered them $50,000. The sisters feared that the house would be torn down to enlarge the amusement park's parking lot. Unhappy at such a possibility, they decided to sell the house for $35,000 to anyone who would save and maintain the property even though this would mean a financial loss to themselves.

A group of Montgomery County, Maryland, Red Cross volunteers met and proposed that the American National Red Cross buy the property and preserve it as a historic site. The Red Cross replied that it could not use its money for such a purpose, that its donations could only go for disaster relief. The Red Cross, however, did enthusiastically support the preservation project and in May 1963 passed a resolution urging all Red Cross members to support the fund-raising effort. On May 28, 1963, this group incorporated itself as the Friends of Clara Barton. They agreed to pay the Frank sisters $1,000 by July 1963 to secure the sale. A whirlwind of bake sales, fashion shows, and other events had raised only $800 by the deadline. Several members went to talk to the Frank sisters to get an extension of the deadline. As they were talking, the amusement park's lawyer walked in and handed one of the sisters a check for $50,000. While they pondered whether to accept the check or grant an extension, one of the Friends ran into the house and burst into the room with a check for $200. The Franks handed the lawyer his $50,000 check and sent him packing.

This was only the initial hurdle, for half of

Red Cross family tree

the remaining $34,000, plus the settlement costs had to be raised by January 1, 1964. Public solicitation, two house tours, and two benefits raised the amount and at the turn of the year the Friends took possession. Later the group bought all of Clara Barton's furniture in the sisters' possession.

In the succeeding years the Friends continued to raise money and work on the house to repair structural defects. In April 1965 the house was designated a registered national landmark. The Friends made their final payment on the mortgage in early 1975. In April they presented the deed to the National Park Service in accordance with legislation passed by Congress in October 1974 authorizing the establishment of Clara Barton National Historic Site.

In December 1979 the Friends disbanded and donated the $8,435.37 remaining in their treasury to the park to purchase furnishings for the Red Cross Offices in the house. Their generosity contributed substantially to the preservation of this property and ensured its survival.

Since acquiring the property, the National Park Service has done extensive research on the building and its contents to determine the proper course of the preservation efforts. Today, work continues on the building and on acquiring furnishings that reflect these findings.

The process of restoration is simultaneously tedious and fascinating. Bit by bit the materials—wallpaper, partitions, even bathrooms—added after Clara Barton's time are removed, revealing the original fabric of the building. Newspapers found in the walls as insulation are removed, flattened, and saved. Historic floors, 1908 electrical wiring, and doorways reappear. New questions arise as old ones are answered. The sources are the house itself, Clara Barton's diary and other writings, and a collection of historic photographs. Each source adds a different perspective to the restoration of her home and to a better understanding of her life.

Clara Barton National Historic Site is open for guided tours on a limited basis. For details call 301-492-6245. Free parking is available. The park offers a variety of special programs on Clara Barton and her times.

Diary and first aid kit

Andersonville National Historic Site, Andersonville, Georgia 31711. The park is the site of the Confederate prison camp for Union prisoners of war. In 1865 Clara Barton met Dorence Atwater, a former prisoner at Andersonville, while she was involved in her search for missing men. Edwin M. Stanton, secretary of war, approved of her plan to go to Andersonville with Atwater and identify as many of the graves as possible. Atwater's written record, which he had kept during his imprisonment, listed each man's name and the number that marked his position in the trench; by comparing this list with the cemetery's numbered markers Barton had no trouble identifying 12,920 graves; 440 remained unknown. During her stay in Andersonville, Barton wrote to Secretary Stanton requesting that the former prison grounds be turned into a national cemetery. Stanton agreed and on August 17, 1865, Barton raised the flag at the dedication.

The park museum contains an exhibit devoted to the work of Barton and Atwater and further explains their role in the establishment of the cemetery. The park is open daily except for January 1, Thanksgiving, and December 25.

Antietam National Battlefield, Box 158, Sharpsburg, Maryland 21782. During the battle of Antietam, Clara Baron attended and helped a Pennsylvania surgeon tend to the Union wounded. The location of this activity has never been precisely determined, though it is known that it did not take place on ground currently owned by the park. Within the park near stop 2 on the driving tour is a monument erected by the Washington County, Maryland, Red Cross chapter in honor of her work during the battle. The park is located north and east of Sharpsburg in west central Maryland and contains the ground on which the bloody September 17, 1862, battle was fought. It is open daily except for January 1, Thanksgiving, and December 25.

Fredericksburg and Spotsylvania County Battlefields Memorial National Military Park, P.O. Box 679, Fredericksburg, Virginia 22401. At Chatham Manor, across the Rappahannock River from Fredericksburg, you can visit the house where Clara Barton provided relief and comfort to the wounded during the battle of Fredericksburg. Exhibits in the Manor about Barton's role include a letter written to a cousin describing the battle scene and her work. Chatham Manor is open daily from 9 a.m. to 5 p.m. It is closed January 1 and December 25. The main visitor center for the park, which contains the battlefields of Fredericksburg, Chancellorsville, the Wilderness, and Spotsylvania Court House, is on U.S. 1 (Lafayette Avenue) in Fredericksburg. A self-guiding automobile tour connects all the battlefields.

Johnstown Flood National Memorial, P.O. Box 247, Cresson, Pennsylvania 16630. The park is located along U.S. 219 and Pa. 869 at the site of the South Fork Dam, 16 kilometers (10 miles) northeast of Johnstown, Pennsylvania. Located at the dam site are a small visitor center, restroom, interpretive trails, and a picnic area with tables and cooking grills. If you drive to Saint Michael on Pa. 869, which closely follows the shore of the 1889 lake, you will pass some of the Queen Anne cottages and the clubhouse that were part of the resort at Lake Conemaugh. Grandview Cemetery in Johnstown contains the graves of many victims, including 777 who were never identified. The park is open daily except Thanksgiving, December 25, and January 1.

Manassas National Battlefield Park, Box 1830, Manassas, Virginia 22110. During the battle of Second Manassas, Clara Barton arrived in Fairfax Station, Virginia, by train with supplies for caring for the wounded. She joined a Federal field hospital that had moved into the hamlet ahead of the Union retreat. At St. Mary's Roman Catholic Church in Fairfax Station the Union doctors set up a hospital. Barton arrived at the same time and contributed medical help. She never reached the battlefield that is preserved in today's park. St. Mary's Church still stands at 11112 Fairfax Station Road, Fairfax Station, Virginia, and a plaque on its wall honors Barton's work.

Eleanor Roosevelt National Historic Site, Hyde Park, New York 12538. Eleanor Roosevelt used "Val-Kill" as a retreat from the cares of her busy and active life. At the cottage, built in 1925 in a pastoral setting, she entertained friends and dignitaries and promoted the many causes in which she was interested.

Maggie L. Walker National Historic Site, c/o Richmond National Battlefield Park, 3215 E. Broad Street, Richmond, Virginia 23223. The brick house at 110A E. Leigh Street was the home of the first woman president of an American bank. She was the daughter of an ex-slave.

Sewall-Belmont House National Historic Site, 144 Constitution Avenue, NE, Washington, D.C. 20002. Since 1929 this house has been the headquarters of the National Woman's Party. It commemorates Alice Paul, a women's suffrage leader and the party's founder, and her associates.

The American National Red Cross Headquarters, 17th between D and E Streets, NW, Washington, D.C. 20006. After Clara Barton resigned as president, the Red Cross needed to find a suitable place for its headquarters. After spending some years in various unused rooms in government office buildings, the U.S. Congress approved legislation that provided $400,-000 to match an equal amount raised privately by Red Cross officials and that donated a city block of land for a building. The land has remained U.S. Government property although it is in the perpetual custody of the American Red Cross. The main building, which fronts on 17th Street, contains exhibit areas on the ground and main floors. A library on the third floor of the office building contains extensive holdings about the Red Cross and related subjects. The complex of buildings is open to the public 8:30 a.m. to 4:45 p.m. Monday through Friday.

Clara Barton Birthplace, 68 Clara Barton Road, North Oxford, Massachusetts 01537. Clara Barton was born in this house on Christmas Day, 1821, the youngest child of Stephen and Sally Barton. The house, which had been built shortly before her birth, is now a museum and contains memorabilia of Clara Barton and her family. The house is open from 1 p.m. to 5 p.m. Tuesday through Saturday in July and August. The remainder of the year it is open only by appointment, primarily for school and private groups. A fee is charged.

Johnstown Flood Museum, 304 Washington Street, Johnstown, Pennsylvania 15901. The museum chronicles the events of the disastrous flood of 1889. Special exhibits detail the role of Clara Barton and the American Red Cross. Here the new organization first demonstrated its ability to respond to a major disaster. The museum continues to work closely with the local chapter of the American Red Cross in maintaining a record of the organization's relief through the years in this flood-prone valley. The museum is open 10 a.m. to 4:30 p.m. Monday to Saturday, and from 12:30 p.m. to 4:30 p.m. on Sundays. It is closed January 1, Memorial Day, July 4, Labor Day, Thanksgiving, and December 25. A fee is charged; group rates are available.

Manuscript Reading Room, Library of Congress, 10 First Street, SE, Washington, D.C. 20540. In the 1930s the Hubbell sisters were doing some remodeling on the Clara Barton House. In the process they discovered a boarded-up corridor between two bedrooms. When the corridor was reopened they found the area filled with Clara Barton's personal papers, diaries, scrapbooks, and other memorabilia of her life and career. Who put them there remains unknown. The two sisters presented the entire cache to the Library of Congress. The collection has been sorted and indexed and is available for the use of scholars only.

Armchair Explorations: Some Books You May Want to Read

Barton, Clara. *A Story of the Red Cross; Glimpses of Field Work.*
New York: D. Appleton and Company, 1904.

_____. *The Story of My Childhood.* New York:
The Baker and Taylor Company, 1907.

Barton, William E. *The Life of Clara Barton.* 2 vols. Boston:
Houghton Mifflin, 1922.

Dulles, Foster Rhea. *The American Red Cross: A History.*
New York: Harper, 1950.

Dunant, Jean-Henri. *A Memory of Solferino.* Washington, D.C.:
The American National Red Cross, 1939.

Fishwick, Marshall. *Illustrious Americans: Clara Barton.*
Morristown, New Jersey: Silver-Burdett, 1966.

Flexner, Eleanor. *Century of Struggle: The Women's
Rights Movement in the United States.* Cambridge:
Harvard University Press, 1974.

Leech, Margaret. *Reveille in Washington, 1860-1865.* New York:
Harper, 1941.

Ross, Ishbel. *Angel of the Battlefield.* New York:
Harper and Brothers, 1956.

☆GPO: 1981 — 341-611/1

Stock Number 024-005-00806-3.

For sale by the Superintendent of Documents,
U.S. Government Printing Office,
Washington, DC 20402.

Index

National Park Service

The National Park Service expresses its appreciation to all those who made the preparation and production of this handbook possible.

Text
Elizabeth Brown Pryor, who wrote Part 2, is a professional historian. She is the author of several journal and magazine articles on nineteenth-century America and lives in Washington, D.C.

Illustrations
The artwork on the cover and on the three double pages introducing the different sections of the book is by Mark English of Fairway, Kansas.
American Red Cross   11 steamboats, 13 Boardman, 39, and 64-65.
Clara Barton Birthplace   76 birthplace.
Johnstown Flood Museum   77 museum.
Library of Congress   8, 9, 10 Anthony, Stanton, and Louise of Baden, 11 Hayes, Garfield, and Arthur, 12 Wald and Adams, 16, 19, 21, 24, 27, 28, 29, 31, 32, 35, 37, 40-41, 43, 44, 46, 51, 53, 56, 60-61.
Museum of Modern Art   59.
New York Public Library   22.
Robert Shafer   68, 69, 71, 75 Sewall-Belmont, 76 American Red Cross, 77 Library of Congress.
Smithsonian Institution   12 ambulance.
All other photographs come from the files of Clara Barton National Historic Site and the National Park Service.